6 95

79-478

79-478

PN155
.H5 Hill, Mary

Into print.

Jefferson College Library
Hillsboro, Mo. 63050

INTO PRINT

INTO PRINT

A Practical Guide to Writing, Illustrating, and Publishing

Mary Hill and
Wendell Cochran

NO LONGER
PROPERTY OF
JEFFERSON
COLLEGE
LIBRARY

Jefferson College Library
Hillsboro, Mo. 63050

William Kaufmann, Inc.
One First Street
Los Altos, California

To William H. Matthews III of Lamar University—geologist, teacher, writer, and photographer, and a fine example of each.

Copyright © 1977 by William Kaufmann, Inc.
All rights reserved. No part of this publication may be reproduced, stored in a retrieval system, or transmitted, in any form or by any means, electronic, mechanical, photocopying, recording, or otherwise, without the prior written permission of the publisher. For further information, write to Permissions, William Kaufmann, Inc., One First Street, Los Altos, CA 94022.

Printed in the United States of America

Library of Congress Cataloging in Publication Data

Hill, Mary, 1923-
Into print.

Includes bibliographical references.
1. Authors and publishers. 2. Illustration of books. I. Cochran, Wendell, joint author. II. Title.
PN155.H5 808 77-4083
ISBN 0-913232-43-2
ISBN 0-913232-44-0 pbk.

CONTENTS

Preface

With this book we hope to prepare you for the ordeal and triumph of publishing. It is a guidebook on how to write what you have to say and how to get it into print.

We've tried to give you guideposts to point the way from initial idea to second edition. For example, our chapters on illustrations will not make you a professional artist, photographer, or cartographer, but they will help you deal with those who are. Virtually every nonfiction work published today contains illustrations, yet it is difficult to find them, to learn how to present them, and to know in what format they should go to the publisher.

We've tried to help you before publication with the trials of writing, organizing, and finding (or becoming) a publisher. The mechanics and processes of typesetting and printing are covered, and we give you directions for proof reading, hints on indexing, and many other useful tips. You will find that publication does not mean completion; you may still have press releases to write, interviews to give, and, of course, a new edition to prepare for.

The center of our target for this book when we began was engineers and scientists of all kinds—physical, biological, natural, social, political. Professional scientists are prolific writers, yet in the field of writing and publishing most of them are amateurs. We hope that scientists and engineers, as well as historians, educators, lawyers, business people, and the many others who write nonfiction will save much time and frustration by using *Into Print.*

Mary Hill
Oakland, California

Wendell Cochran
Arlington, Virginia

September, 1977

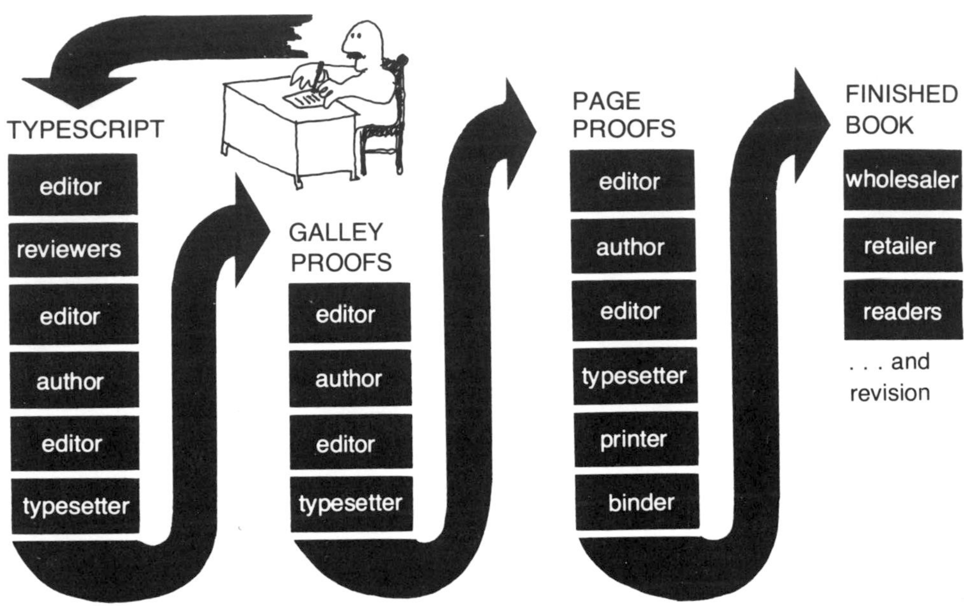

From author to finished book: the ideas move in several forms through many hands.

1 PREVIEWING: looking toward publication

publish or perish?

"Publish or perish," they say. Yet many a writer attempting the former stops now and then to consider whether there is any great risk of the latter. This temptation to forego or delay publication is natural. Most of us find it quite hard enough to master one particular field and so we resist diversion of our time and energy to the complexities of writing, editing, printing, and publishing. Also, some of the skills acquired in the course of producing one article or book may become rusty through disuse and need polishing up for the next one.

However, getting into print is not as hard as it may seem. (Consider the number of books you have read that obviously were written too quickly and published too soon.) If publication looks forbidding, the chances are that you are only unfamiliar with it.

We do not say that getting into print is easy, cheap, and painless. Notoriously, even the best writers are dissatisfied with what they have written and suffer writer's block; and conscientious editors, printers, and publishers all feel the same way about their own work. Each of those professions is complicated and difficult, and the combination is even more so. Nor does modern technology necessarily help: to human errors it may add the errors of the machine.

In short, getting into print (assuming you do it well)

FIGURE 1

requires knowledge, skill, and painstaking work. The route to be traveled by your information—beginning in your mind and ending in the mind of the reader—is likely to be long and full of curves and forks and detours, but the other professionals involved in publishing will make it easier to travel. In this book we will mark the road for you, tell you what hazards to watch for, and suggest ways to deal with them.

consider your audience

Now, a quick survey of the route ahead:

First, what is your goal? Exactly what readers do you want to reach?

what form?

How do you want to send your message? By means of a reference book? a textbook? a technical journal?

which publisher?

Which publisher can help you travel the route? Which one will? Can you agree on mechanical, financial, and legal matters?

along the route

Once you're under way, you'll be guided by an editor. This stage may require considerable seesawing as you propose additions, answer questions, fill in details, excise some passages, insist on finding the phrase that yields your exact meaning, rewrite . . .

Some routes to publication will involve permissions to use photographs or quotations (you could think of them as bridge tolls or travel visas). Remember tax time, and keep financial records in detail.

Somewhere along the route the typesetter will send galley proofs and then page proofs. Check each one carefully and correspond with the typesetter in his own language, through your editor.

nearing the end

As you near the end of the road the printer and binder will take over, but you may still have much to do: indexing, making up your table of contents, recommending journals to receive review copies; checking copy for jacket blurbs or advertising; mailing preprints or reprints . . .

moving on

Finally, you arrive. But what about the next trip? Will you set the same destination? Or travel by the same route? How will you handle reviews, comments by fellow workers, new developments?

key points

On the road to publication

- set your goal
- seek professional help
- take care with details
- look ahead to the next edition

2
RECORDING: keeping track of money and facts

money spent

Tax time is the most obvious reminder to keep records, and the tax collector is the most obvious reason. But tax records are only one kind of record, and in some ways not even the most important.

By all means, keep complete records of money you spend on writing and keep them in order. Keep check stubs, credit-card slips, cancelled checks, cash-register receipts, bills of sale, invoices—everything. Make sure that all of these items are dated and that they show what the money was spent for and where you spent it.

Keep a record of all phone calls you make in regard to your book or article. Record the time, place, and number of each call, plus the name of the person you talked with and notes on the conversation. Such information may help justify a tax deduction. It will help in other ways, too, such as in showing the source of the information that you later decide should be attributed or acknowledged.

rent and equipment

Record money spent for reference books, writing materials, equipment (whether bought or rented), time and space involved in using your home as an office, travel (airline tickets, hotel and restaurant bills, car rental, taxi fares, and so on).

Even if you think an expense will not be deductible, record it. Most likely you are not a tax expert; also, regulations change. Record everything, and as tax time approaches consult a knowledgeable accountant. The worst that can happen (assuming that you are rigidly honest and get good professional advice) is that the tax authority will say no.*

income

After publication, record any payments or royalty income. By having a regular space in your account book for such things, you will notice quickly if an expected payment does not arrive, and you can prod the publisher or query the post office.

literary records

Again, financial records are only the most obvious. Among items that might prove more important are literary records: when you make notes, be sure to write down vital matters such as author's name (*exact* name—never trust your memory), title, edition, year of publication, publisher, page number, physical location (such as New York Public Library). If you can, photocopy the title page and copyright page, or type a detailed file card, or do both.

Double-check to see that you've recorded quotations exactly, and mark them clearly with quotation marks. Plagiarism is embarrassing; copyright infringement is even more embarrassing and can be expensive, too. Whether either is accidental or deliberate doesn't matter much to readers or lawyers, so keep exact records.

permissions

To quote or copy, you must get permission. This is your responsibility, not your publisher's. If you quote from the text or copy an illustration, get permission in writing; do not rely on the phrase "adapted from" to keep you out of trouble. Rules of thumb vary considerably; one publisher specifies that authors must obtain permission if they quote more than five lines of text, but that is a very rough rule and certainly would not suffice for verse or music. When in doubt, get permission.

photographs

Photographs and other illustrations are especially ticklish matters, legally and otherwise. Keep in mind that laws and regulations governing copyright and invasion of privacy are usually more strict for photos than for words. And for your records you may need almost the thousand words a picture is said to be worth; you should have printed slips or rubber stamps so that you can check off, fill in, or cross out (as pertinent) each of these items:

---

*Even if they say no, that isn't necessarily the end. According to an article in the *Wall Street Journal* (July 20, 1977), one scientist-author was allowed by the courts to deduct the expense of a work he published himself even though the Internal Revenue Service had previously barred the deduction.

source—U.S. Bureau of Reclamation [for example]
subject—subsidence of irrigation canal
time and date—3 P.M. November 29, 1976
place—5 kilometers east of Tres Piedras, Fresno County, Calif.
direction—facing west
scale—boulder is 1 meter across
photographer—Susan Moyer
permission or release needed? yes
camera—Nikon F1.
lens—27 mm Nikkor-N Auto 1:2.8, f=24 mm
film—Kodak Tri-X
film rating—ANSI 400
filter—haze
lens opening—*f*16
shutter speed—1/250th second
developer—Dektol
roll number—314
frame number—16

key points

While preparing your manuscript

- record all expenses
- record your sources
- record photo details
- get permissions
- record income after publication

3
WRITING: writing it right

"Easy writing," Ernest Hemingway once said, "makes hard reading." True—but few writers find writing easy. For almost all of us, writing is hard work; it's hard to start writing and it's hard to keep going. No wonder that one author has defined the art of writing as the art of keeping the seat of the trousers in contact with the seat of the chair.

getting started

Books on how to write abound with advice in many forms, and at least one of the many devices suggested should help you—if you find the right one. Some authors can write only while standing; some only in the morning; some only after (and others never after) using recreational chemicals; many only under deadline pressure. But many agree on how to get started: "Get started," one says, citing the first law of motion (a body in motion tends to remain in motion). Another says that "When you can't write, write"—then you can revise and rewrite later and improve almost anything.

However, the first requirement for writing is that you have something to say. The next is that you have a unifying theme, something that holds everything together; otherwise you may be thinking not of one article or book but of two or more.

organizing

If you do have something to say and do have a unifying theme, you must (in nonfiction, at least) already have something down on paper—in papers on your desk, books on your shelves, notes in your files. That is, you have the information in writing; it just isn't organized, clarified, polished, and made plain for your reader. And so your problem of writing becomes largely a problem of organizing.

outlining

Here the logical word is "outline." And outline you must; but there are more ways of outlining than beginning with "I—Introduction" and following with various subsets such as "A," "A1, "A1a," and so on, each with its own indention. The late John Gunther would collect all his notes on separate pieces of paper (he decreed that one rule was inviolable: *never* write on the back of a sheet), spread them around on a long table or the floor, and spend days rearranging them—days, or however long needed to achieve a satisfactory order. That done he found the actual writing comparatively easy.

A simple variation is to write out what you conceive as your chapter titles, each on a separate card, and add other cards as the subjects occur to you (never mind the hierarchical order for the time being) until inspiration fails you. Then use the Gunther method, adding new cards wherever your new order reveals a gap.

writer's block

Finally, start writing. Never mind trying to word your lead sentence exactly right. You don't even have to start at the beginning; write about whatever topic appeals to you most at the moment, switch to another when you must, and fill in the gaps and smooth the transitions as necessary. At first such an erratic course may make you uncomfortable, but if you can't begin at the beginning you must start elsewhere.

Once you've started writing, keep going. Do not stop to seek out the exact shade of meaning or the precise word, or to verify a detail. You can do all those things later, but if you had trouble getting started remember Newton and keep going while you can.

Many writers agree: do *not* keep writing until you reach a logical break such as a chapter end. Either write more or stop short. Then, when you start again the next day you can recapture the flow of words without starting entirely afresh.

Alternatively, you might start a few pages back in what you have already written. Run them through your typewriter again and let inertia carry you past the break.

digging deeper

If you were restricted to only one reference for this chapter, you would do well to start with *Effective Writing for Engineers, Managers, and Scientists* (H.J. Tichy, 1967; John Wiley and Sons, New York). The chapter entitled "Two Dozen Ways to Begin" is an almost certain cure for writer's block—one of the two dozen is sure to give you a way to start writing.

Engineered Report Writing (Melba W. Murray, 1969; Petroleum Publishing Co., Tulsa, Oklahoma) "will help you write good articles and reports more easily and clearly—in your own *best* style." That quotation is from a chapter by Murray in *Geowriting: a Guide to Writing, Editing, and Printing in Earth Science* (edited by Wendell Cochran, Peter Fenner, and Mary Hill, 2nd edition 1974; American Geological Institute, Falls Church, Virginia). Despite its title, you need not be a geologist to understand what it has to say about getting ink onto paper.

Another brief book useful outside the field of its authors is *Scientific Writing* (Lester S. King and Charles G. Roland, 1968; American Medical Association, Chicago); see its chapters "Monotony" and "The Passive Voice." Finally, consider *The Compleat Copywriter* (Hanley Norris, 1966; McGraw-Hill, New York), which is aimed at advertising copywriters—but advertising copywriters know more than almost anyone else about how to deliver a message to the reader's mind.

key points

If you have something to say:

- organize
- outline
- *start writing,* and keep going

4
REWRITING: revising and improving

There's no such thing as good writing, as Justice Louis Brandeis once said, but only good rewriting. That may not be true for *every* writer, but for almost all of us the first draft is only the beginning; it must be followed by changing, correcting, adding, deleting, substituting, polishing—in short, rewriting and re-rewriting.

using a pencil

As much as you can, revise with a pencil. Unless you customarily type a very great deal, a pencil will help you feel closer to your work. A pencil is much more flexible than a typewriter; also, unless you pencil in the changes, you are likely to retype automatically something you meant to improve.

In one sense, rewriting can be dangerous: clearing away unneeded words and the roundabout phrasing required by the passive voice may expose an illogical sequence or a defective thought. "The history of catastrophe," Booth Tarkington once wrote, "is the history of irresistible juxtaposition."

a tool for grammar

However, such simplification is useful in rewriting. In fact, oversimplification is a powerful tool for repairing faulty grammar and the like. Suppose you've found a sentence that seems not quite clear, or one that has an unresolved grammatical problem. Try this: remove all modifiers. Remove all parenthetical expressions. Break up compound sentences into simple sentences. In general, follow Theodore Bernstein's rule of one idea to a sentence. Very often that procedure will isolate the problem and make the solution apparent. After making repairs you can restore the modifiers and the parenthetical expressions and stitch the original sentence together again as far as you see fit.

Finally, let your rewritten work incubate for a few days, or however long you think it might take for you to look at it with a fresh mind. Then edit it with a pencil and run it through your typewriter again.

As rewriting brings you nearer to the final form of your manuscript, you must deal with the matter of "style." But what is "style"? In fact, the term should be taken as a danger flag—a signal to ask "What *kind* of style?" For by that word different writers and editors mean different things at different times. Worse, someone who says "style" may not really have a precise meaning in mind.

four kinds of style

Here is one way to classify style:

1. *Typographic* style consists of the typefaces and other typographic devices consistently used by a given publication; roughly speaking, it is the publication's design. Clearly this kind of style is beyond the writer's control and concern, unless the writer publishes the book himself.

2. *Literary or personal* style, a peculiar and personal matter, is not always apparent—particularly in nonfiction writing. Many writers repress their own style, or imitate others, or lose their own style in compromising with their editors. For others, their styles are like their personalities, simply not obtrusive or otherwise distinctive. We do not mean to imply that there is anything wrong with either the writers' styles or their personalities, for a style should not distract the reader from the content. You must allow your editor to make necessary changes, but take care that the changes do not violate your personal style.

3. *Idiomatic* style consists of distinctions in choice of grammar, syntax, words, and spellings. This style is greatly complicated by levels of usage and by the writer's (and editor's) notion of what is suitable for a given subject and a given publication. In the English-speaking world, editors of formal works tend to settle on H.W. Fowler's *Modern English Usage* as their standard. Although British, *Modern English Usage* is more useful to Americans than many writers and editors realize, and it is far more readable than generally believed.

4. *Editorial or "stylebook"* style, as defined here, re-

fers to the conventions of abbreviation, capitalization, compounding, and the like, as chosen for a given publication. Stylebooks cause much of the confusion about the meaning of "style," for nearly all stylebooks include rules on all kinds of style, often jumbled together almost as if confusion were intended.

sexism Back in the 1960s, "sexism" became an issue to be dealt with by writers and editors, and in writing and rewriting you must take it into account. The intent is plain: it is simply not fair to assume by grammatical implication that a man is superior to a woman, more likely to hold a position of authority, or to follow a given profession (unrelated to actual sex) to the exclusion of women. Or, of course, vice versa.

Few will argue that men and women are not essentially equal, but writers and editors face special problems in dealing with the fact. For one thing, the English language lacks a pronoun commonly used to refer indiscriminately to either sex. Most people feel that "one" in that sense is too pedantic. Some writers have proposed new pronouns such as "shim" or "she/him," but none of those show any sign of gaining acceptance in common speech, and their future in the written literature does not seem promising.

A second problem that well-meaning writers must face is that in avoiding sexist implications they often trap themselves into other faults of writing. For example, you might well object to the sentence "The observer may find it hard to maintain objectivity in his own family;" you might equally object to the roundabout alternative of "In personal family relationships the observer may find it hard to be objective." An acceptable alternative might be direct attribution, as in "Dr. Sharon Free said she would find it hard to be objective if her own family were involved," or, of course, you might quote a man.

Or you might handle it this way: at the first appearance of a troublesome pronoun, indicate parenthetically that you are aware of the implication. Then you can continue with conventional English usage. "When a scientist writes the report, she (or he) must check all references. She must also . . ." Of course the device is good for only a limited space, say one anecdote or one example, and your signal of awareness will not suffice for an entire book.

In any case the objective is to be fair and, as H.W. Fowler said of avoiding an undesirable split infinitive, to "take care to remove all signs of the struggle."

copyediting yourself

Rewriting is do-it-yourself copyediting, and in rewriting you should be anticipating the queries and corrections that would otherwise come later from your editor. You'll find that the list of things to watch for and do is endless, but you can start with these:

Omit needless words. (Look what you can do with "Omit words that are unnecessary.")

Replace long words with short ones. (Avoid "utilization"—use "use"; make up your own list of words to avoid.)

Convert the passive voice to the active. (Most sentences are weakened by the passive form.)

Substitute specific terms for general terms. (Compare "a number of people," "several scientists," and "five biologists.")

Change impersonal nouns to proper nouns. (Not "a peak near the city" but "Mount Diablo, west of Stockton.")

Place words you want to stress at the beginning of the sentence, or at the end. ("I will leave for New York on Wednesday" stresses the day; "I will leave Wednesday for New York" stresses the place.)

Vary sentence lengths. (Variety will help hold the reader's attention, but mere mechanical variation, as in this contrived example, will only call attention to the device.)

Watch your syntax. (Keep in mind that English is basically a distributive language—that the placement of words does much to control the meaning. Where would you place the word "only" in the next sentence? "I hit him in the eye yesterday.")

Remove accidental alliteration, excessive sibilants, and the distractions of rhythm and rhyme (as in those examples).

Break up overlong paragraphs, bearing in mind that you should have one topic to one paragraph.

Check your punctuation. (It affects meaning, and may—at times—indicate the intonations and rhythms of the spoken word. Compare: "I say unto thee, today thou shalt be with me in Paradise" with "I say unto thee today, thou shalt be with me in Paradise.")

Change the nearly right word to the right word. (You should be eager to be precise without being anxious about it.)

Evade sexist implications. (Inordinate and careless use of "he" may suggest that you think all your readers are males.)

Strive for consistent spelling. (If a word is spelled one way on page 9 you should not find it spelt another way on page 88.)

Keep your writing in good taste. ("Guts," rather than "intestines," may be too coarse for your context; on the other hand, not even Victorian tables had "limbs.")

Consider the possibility of libel. (You can say that you disagree with a scientist's results; you should not say or imply that the results suggest incompetence. Be fair.)

permission If you plan to quote more than a very few lines from another published work, you must get permission in writing. This is your responsibility, not your publisher's, and you should get all permissions before your copy goes to the typesetter if only because some copyright holders specify the exact form you must use in giving credit. Most publishers have their own printed forms for authors to use.

PERMISSIONS FORM

July 4, 1976

Rosemary Publications, Inc.
3519 Rosemary St.
Chevy Chase, Maryland 20015

Raymond Street Press is preparing to publish the first edition of *Advertising Production*, by Muriel Barrett. Rosemary Publications gives full permission to Raymond Street Press to use the material described below in its forthcoming publication.

First five lines, page 77, from *Magazine Procedures*, by Elizabeth Groves (1975).

It is (is not) necessary to obtain approval from the author, whose address is

____________ ________________________
date signed

Please send one copy of this release to Permissions Editor, Raymond Street Press.

---

digging deeper

As you rewrite and revise, you will become more and more concerned with consistency of style and with finding exactly the right word to express your meaning. That calls for an editorial stylebook, a dictionary, and a work on English usage.

If your publisher has a house stylebook, get a copy. If there is none, get a good stylebook and make it your own, adapting it as necessary for your special needs. Try the *New York Times Manual of Style and Usage: A Desk Book of Guidelines for Writers and Editors* (edited by Lewis Jordan, 1976; Quadrangle, New York), a dictionary-style guide that tells you under "R" whether the preferred spelling is "Rumania" or "Romania." The *U.S. Government Printing Office Style Manual* (January 1973; Washington, D.C.) is a comprehensive source of style information; it includes such things as non-Roman alphabets, but it is not easy to use and you may find it too complete to be handy. Many writers prefer the University of Chicago's *Manual of Style for Authors, Editors, and Copywriters* (12th edition, 1969; University of Chicago Press), which is the standard for many journals and books, but it is also big and comprehensive.

Desk dictionaries abound. The latest *Webster's New Collegiate* (at this writing, the 1973 edition; G.&C. Merriam Co. Springfield, Mass.) is likely to have the most recent words and definitions. The *American Heritage Dictionary of the English Language* (1973; Houghton Mifflin Co., Boston) takes more care than Merriam to distinguish levels of usage. And *Webster's New World Dictionary of the American Language* (2nd college edition 1970; World Publishing Co.; Cleveland) is especially strong on recent science terms; partly for that reason it is the dictionary adopted by the *New York Times* for its writers and editors.

Now for usage: for half a century *Modern English Usage* (by H.W. Fowler; revised in 1965 by Sir Ernest Gower; Oxford University Press) has been the standard throughout the English-speaking world. It is ubiquitous, authoritative, and comprehensive; those who think it too British for Americans or too forbidding to use simply are not familiar with it.

Nothing can replace Fowler, but there is an excellent American supplement, *The Careful Writer: A Modern Guide to English Usage* (by Theodore M. Bernstein, 1965; Athaneum, New York). This book is based on the experience of many years spent in criticizing the writing and editing for the *New York Times,* and so it deals with the kind of problems you are most likely to find in ordinary writing.

Another useful work on American usage is *A Dictionary of*

Contemporary Usage (by Bergen Evans and Cornelia Evans, 1957; Random House, New York), whose authors often distinguish between British and American usages.

One of the most popular books in this field is "the *little* book"—*The Elements of Style* (by William Strunk Jr., and E.B. White, 2nd edition, 1972; Macmillan, New York). White has revised, and added to, a small textbook used long ago by Professor Strunk at Cornell University. Strunk's chapter on "Elementary Rules of Usage" is rather dated, but "Elementary Principles of Composition" and White's introduction and his "An Approach to Style" will long remain readable and useful to writers and editors.

key points

To improve your manuscript

- edit your typescript, using a pencil
- consider the four kinds of style
- deal with sexism
- rewrite by copy editing
- get permissions

5
REVIEWING: weighing the words of others

If instead of writing a book you are writing a review of a book, you face special problems. Most such problems you can solve by asking yourself "Am I being fair? Is what I've written in good taste?"

fairness and good taste

Obviously it would not be fair for you to review a book if you have any conflict of interest—if, for instance, you contributed to its research, writing, or preparation in any way, or if you were a close friend or associate of the author, or if you and the author are on bad terms with each other.

Less obviously, perhaps, you should not review a book at the request of the author or publisher. Most editors protect themselves and their readers by insisting on soliciting all reviews themselves; some do accept volunteer reviews, but before you write a review, you should inquire.

helping your readers

The main function of a review is to help its readers evaluate the book—that is, to help them decide whether to go to the trouble of finding an actual copy for a closer look. As there are many ways of doing that, there are many kinds of reviews. See your editor's instructions or the journal's examples for guidance, bearing in mind that variety may be acceptable unless expressly forbidden.

kinds of reviews

One kind of review only summarizes the content of the book or gives the range of materials covered. This, the strictly factual review, is especially useful if you think the book badly done but for some reason you don't want to say so explicitly.

Another kind of review restates the author's goal and gives the reviewer's estimate of success in attaining that goal. Another examines the state of the art and places the book in that context. Yet other kinds appraise such topics as the scope of the book, its strengths and weaknesses, its comparability with similar works, its readability, organization, adaptability to various kinds of users, and so on.

systematic checking

Double checking the essential facts about a book you are reviewing is imperative, for the journal editor no longer has the review copy and must rely on you. Make doubly sure of the exact title (from the title page only, as sometimes it appears on the jacket and elsewhere in a slightly different form), the exact name of the author or editor, the name of the publisher, edition if not the first, city and year of publication (use the copyright date), number of text pages, and retail price. Some journal editors also want the number of pages in the front matter (usually in small roman numerals) and the number of figures, plates, and the like.

The journal's style book may specify such matters; if it does not, consult the editor or see a *recent* copy of the journal itself for guidance by example.

You may not have to read every word in a book—particularly one with long tables—before reviewing it, but you must read enough to be sure in your own mind that you are being fair to its author and publisher and to your readers. You must read methodically the table of contents, the foreword (in which the author may indicate the intended readership—an important piece of information often omitted), and the introduction (which should tell the reader how to use the book). Too few people read the front matter. As a reviewer you must not neglect it: all else aside, it will greatly speed your evaluation of the whole.

You may find those approaches obvious and might add others; we list them here mainly to combat a prevalent notion that there is only one kind of review. That notion results in cliché reviews, and clichés within clichés, such as a sort of statistical analysis of pages per chapter, inexpert comments on paper quality, detailed locations of typographical errors, and the too obvious attempt to balance criticisms with forced and insincere praise.

In short: remember your role as agent for potential readers, give the facts, express your honest professional opinion, and be fair.

key points

In reviewing

- be fair
- check details, and recheck details
- give the facts about the book
- dare to be different—there is more than one kind of review

6
PREPARING: typing and labeling the manuscript

When you go for a job interview you naturally try to look your best—you try to lead the interviewer to think something like this: "Here's someone who'll do the job and not cause extra work for me." When you prepare your manuscript to be read or edited you should lead your editor to think something like: "This manuscript won't cause trouble. I won't be distracted by typing errors, and I won't have trouble finding space between lines to mark changes or instructions to the typesetter."

making a good impression

First, your typing should make a good impression, and it will do so if you use a good black ribbon and make as few errors and strikeovers as reasonably possible.

Don't use expensive bond paper, or the kind that has a special coating to make erasing easy. The first is wasteful, and the second will irritate your editor at the first touch of pen or pencil to your manuscript. Whatever paper you propose to use, try it yourself: try it with fountain pen, ballpoint, feltpoint, and lead pencil, making corrections and writing a few words. If any of them blot, smear, blur, or otherwise make trouble in writing or reading, try another paper.

spacing and indenting

Doublespace everything. (Triplespacing is permissible; singlespacing never.) Authors and typists often try to simulate the smaller type of footnotes or quoted matter by singlespacing, but that only annoys editors. Doublespace *everything.*

Use uniform indentation throughout. Here, too, typists often try to anticipate the typesetter, not realizing that they only make it harder for the editor or designer to estimate the space needed on the printed page.

Sometimes authors arrange with their editors to provide machine-readable copy; that is, they type their copy with a special typewriter face (often referred to as OCR for Optical Character Recognition). This can cut costs and speed production, but editor and author must plan extensively beforehand or the results will be added expense and delay. Ask your editor whether it will be workable in your case.

labeling pages

Label and number each page of your manuscript. That may seem to be an elementary reminder, and so it is—it is so elementary that you may easily neglect it and cause trouble for yourself during revision. And just imagine the difficulty if your editor's assistant drops a sheaf of 50 unnumbered pages.

For labeling and numbering pages, one author uses return-address stickers, the kind that you buy printed for a dollar or two per thousand stickers. She buys a separate stack for each of her books, specifying an imprint with her name, a short form of the book's title, the word "chapter" with a space for penciling in the number, and word "page" plus a space. The device is fast and easy and reminds her to number and label each page.

Be sure to keep a copy of your manuscript—a copy that will yield legible photocopies. Often one copy for the publisher will do, but many publishers will want one carbon copy (or photocopy) or more.

Mail your manuscript in a package that will keep it flat and protect the corners of the pages (cardboard or other stiffener may be required).

Do not send art work unless specifically requested, but it may help to include photocopies of the art work at the appropriate places, interleaved in the manuscript.

Consult your postmaster about the manuscript rate for postage, and do enclose a stamped and self-addressed envelope. Enclose, or attach, a letter making clear what is to be done with your manuscript, this depending on the status of your negotiations with the publisher.

Don't worry about copyright at this point. Before Jan. 1, 1978, common law (and sometimes state laws) protects your manuscript from piracy. After that date, the written law incorporates common law in copyright matters, and your work is copyright on creation. However, after publication you (or your publisher) should register the work with the Register of Copyrights, Library of Congress, Washington, D.C. 20559.

digging deeper

Many stylebooks give detailed instructions for typing manuscripts. Among them is the *Manual for Writers of Term Papers, Theses, and Dissertations* (Kate L. Turabian, 3rd edition, 1972; University of Chicago Press), which is based on the University of Chicago's *Manual of Style.* Many individual journals offer sample sheets or booklets of instructions free.

key points

When preparing your manuscript

- be neat and orderly
- choose the right kind of paper
- label everything
- take care in shipping

7 ILLUSTRATING: evaluating kinds of illustrations

pictures versus words

Almost every nonfiction published work, whether it is a highly technical paper for a scientific journal or the stockholders' report of a business, uses illustrations. Indeed, since the middle of the 20th century, graphics—including film and television—have assumed an increasingly large role in our everyday lives, with a correspondingly smaller role for the written word. You need to consider your graphics carefully, for they are likely to be at least an equal partner with words in your published work.

Nevertheless, before choosing any kind of graphic illustration, ask yourself: "Will a picture make this clearer than words?" If it will not, then do not take the trouble to make the illustration.

For graphic art work is a lot of trouble. Very few writers are competent enough artists, cartographers, or photographers to make illustrations of publication quality. You will probably need a specialist to help you with most of the visual material, but no one can help you efficiently if you do not know what you want. You should be familiar with all kinds of graphic presentations so that you will be able to select the most effective one for your purpose, and to instruct the artist in what you need.

which kind of illustration?

Once you have decided that you do need an illustration, you must choose which kind of illustration is most suitable.

If "who" or "what" can be shown clearly in a photograph, that may be your best choice. If not, then a photograph combined with art work, or a drawing alone, may be best.

If you have numbers too awkward for the text, choose a chart or table, for these show "how much." If you wish to show "where" (perhaps combined with how much), draw a map; if you need to show "how," make a diagram.

After you have determined which kind is best, and have worked with your graphic artist enough to plan the illustration, then be available for consultation, but allow the artist freedom to do the best work he can. After all, he or she is an expert in that field, and can best help you by being allowed to do so. Nevertheless, watch progress carefully, and, if you can, tread the narrow line between observing progress and standing over your artist. An experienced graphic artist should know more about publication methods than you do, but not all artists will. Try to select one who does; but if you do not, or cannot, make certain that he or she understands what is required for printer's copy.

size and shape

You cannot give exact instructions regarding the size and shape of illustrations until you know the size of the printed page. When you do (professional journals will send this information to you on request), you can see how large an illustration must be if it is to be reduced in the printing process. The chart in Figure 2 shows a graphic method of calculating reduction.

Although you cannot determine the exact size of all of your illustrations—your publisher has the final say—you can submit illustrations of a suitable shape. Some of them, particularly photographs, when printed may cover the entire page or have no margin on one or more sides. Illustrations that have no margin are known as "bleed" illustrations. Although the selection of illustrations to be bled is not your final decision, you can indicate those that you think would be enhanced by this treatment. They must have an extra ⅛ inch (3 mm) of photograph or drawing on all sides that are to be bled. You would not, of course, choose to bleed any illustration that has an inked border.

If you can possibly do so, arrange all of the illustrations that have numbers or words on them (particularly graphs, charts, tables, drawings, and diagrams) to fit a page vertically. This is the easiest for readers, causing the least disruption in reading. It also makes comparison of the chart with the text possible. This arrangement will also prevent lettering on illustrations from appearing upside down, when

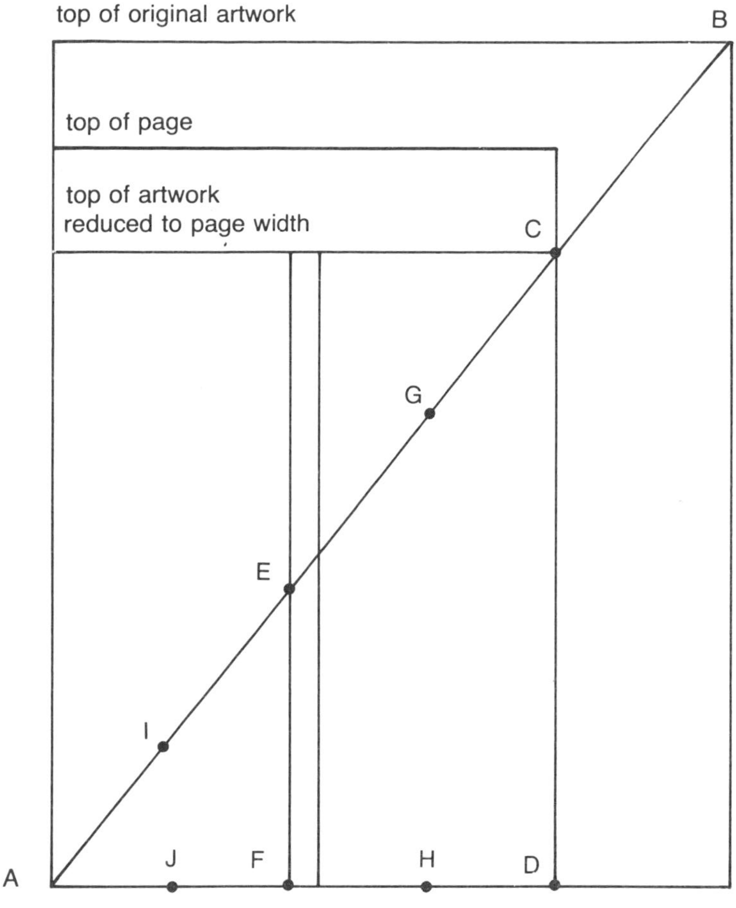

One method of figuring reductions. FIGURE 2

the book is held vertically, as it sometimes must if figures are prepared for printing broadside.

Your artist or cartographer will need to know what size and shape to plan illustrations before making them. If you already have a publisher, ask for instructions as to the shape of the page, the amount of space on a page usable for illustrations, and how much he intends to reduce the illustrations. If you do not yet have a publisher, you would be wise to make neat pencil sketches of your art work, but do not complete them until you have information on format.

If you are writing for a science journal, write to the editor asking how to submit illustrations. You will be asked to submit finished drawings with your manuscript, but do not complete them until you know what is required.

Almost all publishers and journal editors ask that art work be planned to be printed smaller than the original drawing or photograph, so as to take advantage of the sharpening and smoothing that reduction gives. Lettering and lines must be heavy enough to reduce without fading, yet light enough that areas are not plugged by spreading ink. Figure 3 shows a line drawing and lettering at different amounts of reduction.

lettering

Lettering for art work can be good freehand, mechanical, printed, or adhesive. Freehand lettering, when done by an artist, is the most pleasing, but, like printing, expensive. Mechanical methods, such as Wrico and Leroy, are clear and suitable, but do not have the variety that is now available in adhesive sheets or by cold-type composition (see page 129). Art and engineering supply stores stock many different styles of alphabets, sizes of type, and designs for use in preparing art for printing. Or, individual words or whole pages can be set in hot type (see page 129)

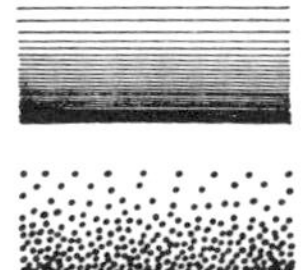
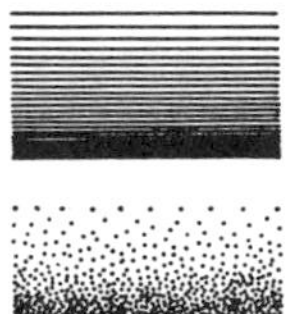
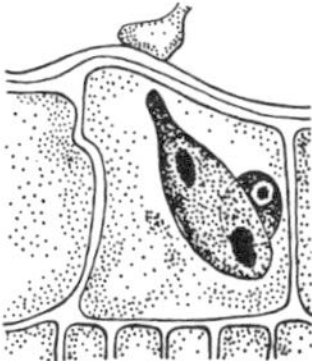
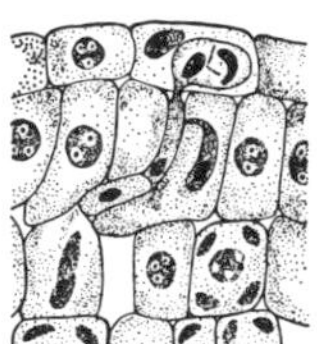
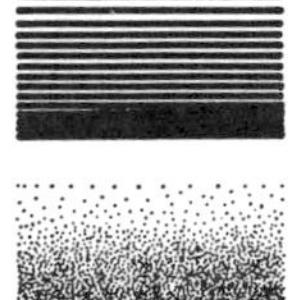
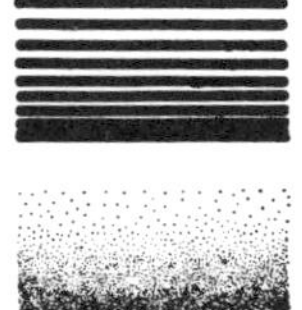

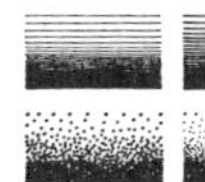
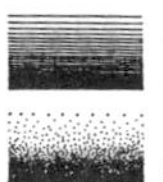
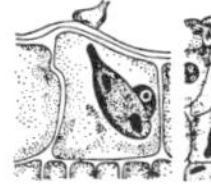
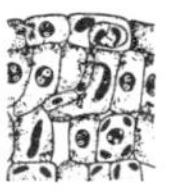
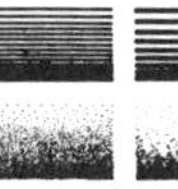

FIGURE 3 Letters, lines, and dots as they appear after reduction on the printed page. Top, the original art; lower left, the art has been reduced to half size; lower right, to a quarter of its original size. Some detail has been lost and some details "plugged" by ink as the art is reduced.

to be printed on adhesive sheets. It is quicker and less expensive, however, to set words or phrases on a cold-type composition machine. Some such machines, like their hot-type counterparts, can set entire pages for your artist to use, in a choice of type style and size.

Each composite piece of art must have registration marks (+ or ⊕), for each part, which should be placed outside the margins so that they will not show when printed.

caring for illustrations

For every part of every piece of art work, follow these rules:

Never paste art work in the manuscript; always submit it separately.
Never write on the face of any illustration; always use an overlay with registration marks.
Never write on the back of any illustration. Ink and pencil may show through as colors or indentations.
Never put figure numbers on the face of the illustrations or the overlays. They may be renumbered by the publisher. Identify illustrations on a separate sheet attached lightly to the illustration on its reverse side, or included separately in an envelope with the illustration (see page 50 for more details on identifying illustrations).
Never use paper clips or staples.
Never roll illustrations. Always ship them flat, in a sturdy box—a wooden crate if necessary.

labeling art

No matter how many, how few, or how diverse your illustrations, each piece must be clearly identified with its own label that gives the illustration numbers, your name, and the subject of your manuscript. Although you must provide detail about each one (including a caption), the minimum that must appear on each piece of art work, and on each separate part of composite pieces, must be something like this:

Figure 1
Hill and Cochran
Into Print

In addition, you should mark in the text where each piece of art should be printed, if it is to appear with the typeset copy. Bear in mind that, for reasons of design, the art may not appear exactly where you wish.

If you have photographs or art work to be printed in color, drawings that will be larger than a full page, or a great many photographs, consult your publisher for ways to deal with them. Maps, when printed, can be folded in a pocket; color photographs may be grouped together in one place. If you cannot find out how you should indicate where oversize or unusual art work should go, you can mark its place, too, in the text, but do not be disappointed if it is not printed exactly where you indicate.

permissions

If you borrow illustrations from other sources, including published sources, you should obtain permission to use them. It is mandatory to request permission to reprint copyrighted illustrations, it is courteous to request permission from such noncopyright sources as the U.S. government. You need not seek permission for illustrations that are in the public domain by reason of their age, but be safe.

credits

Whether permission is required or not, you should acknowledge the source by a suitable credit line, even if you have paid for the use of the illustration. The exact wording may be specified when permission is granted, or you may be allowed to write the acknowledgment yourself. You and your publisher can decide whether to include this information as part of the caption, or to group all credits together in one place. The important point is that you do acknowledge the source.

You should also give credit to the artists and others who prepared the new material for your publication. Even if you never see a bill for their services—perhaps your publisher or your company pays—they have invested time and interest in your project. Again, you can handle this illustration by illustration, acknowledging the creator on each piece of art or in its caption, or you can include such credits in your "Acknowledgments" section. If someone prepared a large number of new illustrations for your publication, you should consider placing the artist's name on the title page or in the heading, something like as this:

TRILOBITE DISEASES
By Charles F. Smith
Illustrations by Henrietta Smith

Do not feel that sharing the limelight in any way diminishes your contribution. On the contrary, it establishes you as someone more interested in your subject—and its best possible presentation—than in yourself. And that, after all, marks a professional.

digging deeper

Steps toward Better Scientific Illustrations, by Arly Allen (Allen Press, 1976; Lawrence, Kansas) and *Artist's Market* (published annually by Writer's Digest, Cincinnati, Ohio) are helpful to authors; so is *Printing It,* by Clifford Burke (Wingbow Press, Berkeley, California). Books that will help with specific illustration problems are listed in the chapters following.

key points

Prepare illustrations—if showing is better than telling

- select the form of illustration best suited to your subject
  - photographs and drawings show who or what
  - charts and tables show how much
  - maps show where
  - diagrams show how
- identify all parts of illustrations
- indicate where illustrations go in manuscript
- get permissions
- credit sources

8 PHOTOGRAPHING: selecting camera and film

kinds of cameras There are no restrictions on the kind of camera you use to make photographs for publication if it can make a sufficiently clear image to produce illustrations of good quality. As photographs for scientific purposes usually emphasize detail, you will need a camera with a lens capable of high resolution. Although you can take landscape photographs with a camera that has a viewfinder, for most scientific purposes you will be so close to the subject that unless you take this closeness into account (the effect is called "parallax"), the top part of your subject may not be included in the photograph. For that reason, you will find it easier to use cameras with arrangements for viewing directly through the lens (single-lens reflex or view cameras).

negatives The size of the negative determines the size of the camera; the larger the negative, the less the photograph will need to be enlarged for publication. As each increment of enlargement renders the photograph less clear, it follows that the larger the negative the sharper the final printed product. However, you need not use a huge camera to get results that are adequate for publication, as modern lenses and films are of high enough quality that a moderate-size negative (5 cm by 5 cm, for example) will yield excellent results if you take care in making it.

film Two kinds of film sensitive to visible light are used for science publication: color, and black and white. Of these, black and white is still the more commonly used, principally because it can be printed much more cheaply than color.

black and white

Many manufacturers in many countries make black-and-white film. There are many brands, and many types of each. Each has its own characteristics, and you must study them carefully to control results. Professional photographers commonly select two or three types of film and learn them well, rather than constantly shopping among the hundreds available.

Continuous-tone emulsion film and high-contrast (monotone) emulsion film are the two basic black-and-white types best for publication. Emulsion-coated glass plates, still used (although rarely) for lantern slides, are no longer used for general photography.

Continuous-tone emulsion film is best known to most people, as it is the black-and-white film available at tourist shops and general merchandise stores. It produces an image having a range of tones from black to white with many shades of gray between. It is available as panchromatic film, which will render all colors of the visible spectrum as some shade of gray, black, or white, and as color-blind film, which does not register certain colors. The latter films, called "orthochromatic," are useful for such special purposes as portraits of men, and each can be developed by visual inspection under a safelight of whatever color the film is blind to. The more common panchromatic films must be developed in total darkness, as all visible colors produce an image upon them.

Black-and-white and color continuous-tone film that provides a print almost instantaneously is also available, but must be used in special cameras or special camera backs. The advantage of an immediate print is that failure can be remedied at once, but this kind of film has the disadvantage of providing only one print. Some "instant" films yield a negative, but they require special equipment and immediate processing. Such prints can be copied, thereby providing a negative for enlargement, but all copy work erodes quality.

The best use of instant film in publishing is as a preliminary check on lighting, exposure, composition, and approximate tonal values, before making a conventional negative.

Monotone film, which renders all light of any color as black or white (there are no grays), has special uses in science photography and publication. Such film is used in reproducing line drawings and other art work, where no gray tones are required. It is also used in producing the effect of gray in the halftone printing process. In this process, a continuous-tone photograph is rephotographed using monotone negative material. By imposing a "screen," or dot or line pattern, between the monotone film and the continuous-tone original, the effect of continuous tone can be reproduced in the printed book (see page 129). Monotone film is not well known to most photographers, as its principal use is in publication, but if you are familiar with its characteristics, you can use it for other special purposes, too.

"speed" and f stops

Film is available for all sizes of cameras, but not all kinds of film are made in all negative sizes. One decision that you must make immediately in choosing a film to use is what "film speed" you need. This, in turn, will limit the types of film available to you. Film speed, expressed as ANSI (American National Standards Institute—formerly ASA, American Standards Association) or DIN (Deutsche Industrie Norm) ratings, is a measure of the amount of light necessary to make an acceptable image. The higher the ANSI (ASA) or DIN number, the "faster" the film; that is, the less light will be required for the photograph. Therefore, where little light is available, a high film speed is needed.

The problem would be simple if you had only to match film speed with light, but other factors intervene. In general, the faster the film, the lower its ability to reproduce fine detail (that is, the faster the film, the grainier the image); for that reason, most photographs intended for science publication are made on fairly "slow" film (low ANSI or DIN rating) if possible.

Another factor in dealing with the problem of light and film speed is the lens opening (the "*f*" stop) to be used, as the larger the *f* stop (in this case, the smaller the *f* number), the less of the image will be in focus. A lens opening of *f* 2.8, for example, is larger in diameter, but it will have a smaller range in focus from foreground to background than *f* 32.

For many purposes, it is best to have only a narrow range from foreground to background in sharp focus. For example, in photographing an ant in a garden, you would probably want the ant to be sharp and clear, with the background plants and leaves merely a backdrop. The end result must be considered before the photograph is made, and preferably before a kind of film is chosen.

color

Films that render an image in approximately natural color are of two basic kinds: those that produce a negative, from which color prints can be made, and those in which the film itself becomes transparent during development.

Either negative or transparent film can be used for illustrations in books and magazines, but many publishers have a preference. Color photographic prints are sometimes acceptable, if carefully done, but your publisher may ask you for the negative, too. If you submit negatives or transparencies to your publisher, take great care to identify and protect them, as they are unique and therefore irreplaceable.

Color illustrations are an exception to the rule that photographs should be submitted at an enlarged size. If possible, color photographs should be submitted at printing size. Generally this is not possible, because transparencies are submitted more often than prints. The reason is that film for transparencies is finer grained; and because of the manner of its construction, transparency film makes better printed illustrations than color-negative materials.

As color perceived varies with the conditions under which we perceive it, some printers ask authors to submit a notation regarding the best light intensity for viewing the transparency to obtain true color. An alternative is to have a color print made that has accurate color to serve as a printer's guide. Transparencies should be clearly marked as to which is the top, either by a tiny notch in the film itself or by an india-ink mark in the border of the film. As mountings may be removed by the printer, it is no use to indicate "top" on a cardboard mount. Each transparency should be packed in an individual glassine envelope.

It is possible, of course, to make duplicates of transparencies and negatives. As there is always some change in color and loss of clarity, avoid copying if you can.

color rendition

Color rendition is a complex problem, as many factors affect it. The "color temperature" (as measured by a meter) of the light source is of primary importance. For example, the color temperature (expressed in degrees Kelvin), and therefore the hue, varies according to the angle of the Sun. It follows, then, that the dominant color of light is different from morning to night and from winter to summer, as well as being of a different quality at different latitudes. You would not normally eliminate natural-light variations, even if you could, as they add artistic interest to your work. Of course you should be careful that great differences in light do not portray your subject incorrectly.

In photographing artificially lit subjects, too, color rendition is affected by the color temperature of the lights you use, and the color temperature itself can be altered by changes in line voltage of your source, or by an electrical cord whose wire is not heavy enough.

In addition to the color of the subject and the color of the light, the color of the photograph is affected by the color-rendering characteristics of each kind and brand of film. As in black-and-white photography, it is wise to become thoroughly familiar with one or two kinds of film. Development and printing, also, can and do change the hues rendered.

Even after you have obtained a suitable color photograph to supply your publisher, the battle for accurate color rendition is not over. Your publisher—perhaps with your help or that of your artist or photographer—will make color separations from your photographs (see page 130). If that is not carefully and accurately done, the printed color may be untrue. In the printing process itself are many other pitfalls: the printer must choose colors of ink to match the colors of the photographs; he must see that they are distributed properly on the printing plate; he must recognize that the kind and condition of his machinery, as well as the temperature and humidity of the press room, all affect color rendition.

However, not all color photography is required to be true color. Certain types of film, infrared and thermal infrared, for example, present subjects in "false" colors. Infrared is particularly helpful in delineating vegetation and rock types, and thermal infrared has been used for such purposes as detecting water pollution and prospecting for mineral deposits.

satellite images

Images from cameras mounted in space satellites have opened a new field of illustration and research. The techniques are called "remote sensing" and the products are called "images" rather than photographs because they do not necessarily use materials sensitive to visible light. They are more closely related to television pictures than to conventional photographs. When different parts of the electromagnetic spectrum are used as well as visible light, what appear to be wholly different views result. Each image contains millions of tiny "dots" of information (picture elements) called "pixels," each pixel showing approximately 1.1 acres (about 4,500 square meters) of ground surface, or an area about the size of a football field. Pixels can be analyzed, "enhanced," and corrected by computer. The results, which can be printed on light-sensitive photographic paper, give astonishing pictures of Earth and other planets, as well as opening new fields of scientific inquiry.

digging deeper

See pages 41-42.

key points

When you select your photographic tools

- choose a camera large enough to make an adequate negative
- choose a kind of camera that will allow accurate viewing
- select film with publication in mind

9
LIGHTING: illuminating the subject

direct sunlight Lighting for outdoor photography depends in large part upon the Sun. Direct overhead noon lighting is rarely suitable, as shadows are necessary to show relief. Sun angles closer to the horizon provide more interesting light; in fact, some Earth features become clear only when the Sun has barely risen or is near setting—but sunlight is redder at these times. Study the subject carefully and wait for the best light.

Lighting for outdoor photographs in which the subject is fairly close, perhaps within 20 feet (6 meters), can be enhanced by judicious use of a flash unit or reflectors. For example, a subject may be nicely outlined, even haloed, by back lighting (the Sun facing the camera), but details will not show. The photograph, if no additional light is directed on the side of the subject facing the camera, will be a silhouette of the subject.

"limbo" Many photographs for scientific publication are made under controlled conditions, in the studio or laboratory, where the lighting can be carefully arranged to show the subject best. Common subjects are artifacts, art objects, botanical, zoological, medical, and geologic specimens, cultures, and prepared materials. In photographing these objects, as well as small subjects outdoors, you must devise a way to isolate the subject from its background. On the television screen, a person may appear to be standing alone in space, surrounded by darkness. Such lighting is called "limbo" in television parlance. It is this effect the photographer of science specimens will often wish to reproduce: the subject, its relief sharply etched, yet divorced from a recognizable background so that the viewer's attention is focused on specific details of the subject. At times, of course, you may wish to show the subject in its natural setting, but you should remember that the background details may vie with the subject for interest.

studio lighting

Isolation is easiest to achieve by eliminating distracting objects from the background. Use a plain white backdrop (card or cloth) or a solid black one for black-and-white photographs. Black is dramatic but difficult to publish, as the halftone printing process yields a rich black only if the printer takes great care. Avoid gray backgrounds, as they tend to become muddy in printing. For color photography, brightly colored backgrounds are exciting, but the brilliance of their color may draw attention away from the subject, or may, if carelessly used, give a false impression of the color of the subject. Pastel, black, and off-white are good for this purpose. Choose a background that will show the subject well.

Several excellent works on studio lighting have been published. Although you should consult them before beginning a project in studio photography, experience is indispensable. You can save time at this stage by making an instant print as an immediate test of your lighting setup.

sources of light

Whatever your lighting arrangement, you need to know the quantity and distribution of light, which you can determine only by judicious use of a sensitive light meter. If you are working in color, you will also need to know the color temperature, which you can discover by special measurement or by calculation of the temperature and quantity of all your light sources (consult the manufacturer's specifications for each piece of your lighting equipment).

The sources of light for microscopic photography are more limited than for many other kinds of photography. For some microscopic specimens, only transmitted light passing through the subject can be used; some are lighted only by light falling on the microscope stage. In either case, the quantity of light will be small, and the length of time required for exposure of the negative proportionately large. Be sure to indicate in the caption any unusual feature of the light in your photomicrograph. If the subject was photographed under polarized light or cross-polarized light (crossed nicols), say so.

Longer exposures are also required for the subjects that may be seen through telescopes. Here, you have virtually no control over lighting; you must photograph astronomical subjects by their own light, and you cannot control the light falling on Earth-bound subjects photographed through a telescope.

Some other subjects, photographed under conditions where you cannot physically move them, or control the background or the lighting, can be isolated by selecting a lens opening that will provide a narrow range of focus (small depth of field). Such photographs show the subject in sharp focus, the background as a general blur.

scale

Photographs for science publication should have some indication of scale. This scale need not always be stated: in a photograph of a mountain range, or a close-up of a praying mantis, the size is well known. However, for most subjects, scale should be implied by comparison with known objects in the photograph, or expressed by graphic or mathematical methods, or in words.

Beware of concerning yourself with scale to the detriment of the subject. We often see photographs of small objects posed beside wooden rulers, in which the ruler so dominates the photograph that the subject is lost.

Close-up photography (macrophotography) poses other problems of scale. Generally, close-up work is done with special lenses, bellows, or tubes, or any combination attached to a conventional camera. It is a useful technique for portraying objects of small but not microscopic size. It can be used outdoors for photography of such small subjects as insects in their natural setting, or in the studio or laboratory to photograph artifacts and mineral specimens.

A subject of a close-up photograph is shown from approximately one-tenth to about ten times its natural size. Although it is possible to include a natural scale in the photograph, it is rarely desirable. An oak, for example, might serve well as an indicator of scale in landscape photography, but acorns probably have too great a range in size to be helpful for close-ups. You can, of course, provide a graphic scale to accompany the photograph (don't draw on the print; use an overlay), but a more artistic solution is a verbal or mathematical scale. "Specimen is 3 mm long" will convey the needed information with least disturbance to the composition of the photograph.

If you use a mathematical scale ("x10"), be certain to take into account the magnification of the subject on the negative and the enlargement of the print. The editor and printer must be careful to maintain the same scale or alter the statement to fit the size of the printed subject. As the author you must make certain it has been done correctly.

In using photomicrographs (photographs made through a microscope), you will rely entirely upon graphic or verbal

FIGURE 4

Scanning electron micrograph of ash from the 1976 eruption of Augustine Volcano, Alaska, showing one method of indicating scale. The white "tick" marks along the bottom of the photograph mark 30-micrometer (0.0012-inch) intervals. Magnification is 640 times. The white box surrounds an area 75 micrometers by 60 micrometers (0.003 by 0.002 inches) that was further enlarged 3,200 times. The enlargement can appear as a separate figure, or this or the enlargement can serve as an inset. In printing, the identification numbers and letters in the margin would be cropped. Polaroid negative film was used for this figure.

scales. The same caution applies in computing the scale: remember to account for magnification by the microscope, magnification by the camera lens, magnification by the enlarger, and scale changes in printing. For such minute objects as those photographed by the scanning electron microscope, a mathematical scale is probably best, as it is very difficult to convey an idea of size in words when magnification may reach 100,000 times.

standards for magnification

Although it is not mandatory, the American Society for Testing & Materials, which sets standards for various purposes, recommends that these magnifications be used

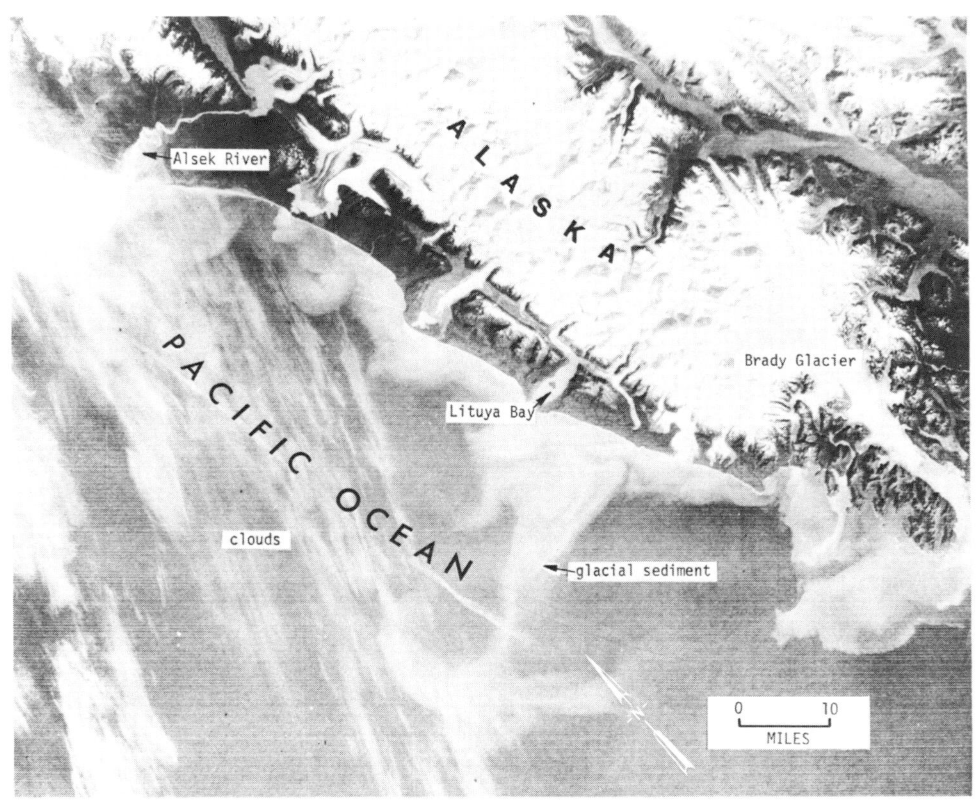

FIGURE 5 Image from the first experimental Earth Resources Technology Satellite (ERTS-1), revealing sediment plumes from coastal glaciers of Alaska. The plumes can be clearly identified, extending more than 30 miles into the Pacific Ocean. Here a graphic scale is given, and prominent geographic points are identified. This figure covers an area approximately 400,000,000 times as large as that shown in Figure 4.

to allow the viewer to compare sizes more easily: 5x, 10x, 25x, 50x, 75x, 100x, 150x, 200x, 250x, 500x, 750x, 1,000x, 1,500x, 2,000x.

The special scale problems encountered in presenting X-ray photographs, underwater photographs, and photographs made by other less conventional methods can all be solved by including size information in the caption. This is probably the best solution, too, for giving readers an idea of scale in aerial photographs and in images made for remote-sensing purposes. The size of the subject in a photograph of the entire ball of Earth, taken from space, is as clear to us from the photograph as words could be, but a view of part of the surface from several hundred miles up can be more puzzling. Such images (as for example the many available from satellites), so helpful in research, will need to be "scaled" if they are to be used for illustration. A mathematical scale (for example, 1:250,000) is most accurate, if it can be calculated (again, beware of changes of size in printing), or if it cannot, a statement such as "The Red Sea is shown at upper left" indicates to the reader the area involved.

digging deeper

Photography is a profession in its own right, and its literature is vast. If you are a scientist you may find much of the information you need in various handbooks published by Eastman Kodak. Each year, the company prints an index to its published works; a current copy of the *Index* may be obtained by writing to Eastman Kodak Company, 343 State Street, Rochester, New York 14650.

Landscape photographer Ansel Adams has written a very helpful series of books. The scientist will find technical assistance in *Camera and Lens, The Negative, The Print, Natural-light Photography,* and *Artificial-light Photography,* all published by Morgan and Morgan, Hastings-on-Hudson, New York.

The Life Library of Photography (Time-Life Books, New York) is a superb reference series, particularly for those who like well-chosen and well-printed examples. The volume entitled *Photographing Nature* (1971) deals with close-up, landscape, and underwater photography, as well as animal and plant illustration. *Light and Film* (1970) tells much about film and exposure, light, and lighting. *Color* (1970) and *The Camera* (1970) discuss those subjects in words and pictures. This series makes excellent reading, too.

For field use, a handy, ready reference is *Handbook of Nature Photography,* a Sierra Club Totebook, written by Patricia Maye (1974).

Two other very helpful books are *Photography for Scientific Publication* (1965) and *Field Photography, Beginning and Advanced Techniques* (1976), both by Alfred A. Blaker (W.H. Freeman and Company, San Francisco). Blaker gives solutions to many particular problems encountered in photographing material in the museum, studio, and laboratory.

In addition to these and many other books and articles on photography, there are good manuals for use with particular cameras. For example, *Graphic Graflex Photography* (Morgan and Lester, 1947) deals with view and press cameras, *The Hasselblad Way* and *Nikon F Nikkormat Handbook of Photography* with methods of using those cameras and equipment made for them.

Reference material on remote sensing is accumulating rapidly. Ask your librarian to help you with references on this subject—or any of the others—if you need them.

key points

In making photographs for publication

- arrange lighting and background to enhance your subject
- compute mathematical scale or supply graphic scale
- prepare photographic prints of density, size, and surface for maximum clarity

10 SEARCHING: making, finding, and handling photographs

Cleanliness, neatness, and care are watchwords with all art work. Because all of us can and do take photographs, they have become the form of art work that is most mistreated. It takes time and care to produce professional results, and time and care to present the photographs best to your readers.

studying your subject

If you plan to take your own photographs, study your subject carefully. Even if you have spent a lifetime in academic research on your subject, you may not yet have studied it with photography in mind. Do so; become intimate with your subject—study it closely and get as close as possible to photograph it. Most nonprofessional photographers stay too far from their subjects, and are too quick to trip the shutter.

composition

Learn the principles of composition as they apply to photography. After all, the principles of art apply to every illustration, whether it is published in a scientific document or displayed in an exhibition. Helpful books on composition may be obtained from your library or purchased in inexpensive editions. Some are mentioned on pages 41-42 and 53.

finding existing photographs

If you wish to use photographic illustrations, and do not have your own, you can obtain photographs from many sources. If you are writing a paper for a scientific journal or a freelance article prepared without previous arrangement with a publisher, you will probably be required to submit all illustrations in a completed form, including photographs. If you are writing a textbook or other nonfiction work on contract or on assignment, your publisher may help you obtain photographic illustrations.

Among the many sources for photographs are federal and state agencies and archives (for example, the U.S. Department of Agriculture, the National Aeronautics and Space Administration, and the Library of Congress), chambers of commerce, business and professional photographers, as well as colleagues and friends. Generally, government sources charge nominal fees to cover their costs, or do not charge at all; firms whose products are exhibited usually provide prints free; professional photographers and agencies charge professional fees. The fee may vary according to the use you make of the photograph; that is, whether you wish to publish it one time or several, whether it is to be used for advertising or not, or whether you ask for international rights, television rights, or have other uses in mind.

permissions

In soliciting photographs for publication, you should make clear what use you intend, so that when you receive the prints you will have the right to publish them. Allow plenty of time to obtain your photographs. It takes time for even a professional photographer who already has a suitable negative, well indexed, to find it and make a good print. Photographic agencies and professional photographers will probably specify, in their reply to you, what rights you have purchased, if they differ from what you have requested (for example, "one-time use only"). If you have stated your intent to publish in your request, any photographs you receive from government agencies, industrial firms, and other non-professional photographic sources will probably not require further permission to publish. To be on the safe side, it is wise to use a form such as the one shown on page 45. This should be sent in duplicate, so that one copy can be returned to you and one retained by the source.

If you have paid to have your photographs prepared or have taken them yourself, they are yours to publish as you wish. Nevertheless, owning publication rights to the photographs does not mean that you can publish without regard for what is contained in the photograph. Probably you can, if there are no people in it and if you do not use it for advertising purposes. For most nonfiction works, the law protecting the right to publish photographs of an education-

SAMPLE LETTER FOR REQUESTING PERMISSION TO USE PREVIOUSLY PUBLISHED PHOTOGRAPHS

Dear [Publisher] :

May I have your permission to use the photograph listed below [or of which a photocopy is attached] in a book [or article] on [subject of book or article] that I am writing, to be published by [name of publisher or journal]?

From [Cite where you saw the photograph. If a book, author and title; if journal, cite journal, article, author, volume, number, page, figure number, and date].

I would like nonexclusive rights to use this photograph; I will, of course, see that an acknowledgment is published in the book [or article].

As a satisfactory reproduction can be made only from a glossy print, can you supply me with one [or them] or tell me where it [or they] may be obtained? [Omit this paragraph if you know the source and are writing to it separately.]

I will greatly appreciate your prompt consideration of my request. The form at the bottom of this sheet is for your reply; the duplicate is for your records.

Sincerely yours,

You have our permission to use the illustrations[s] listed above.

____
Date

____
Signature

____
Publisher

al or informative nature will cover even photographs of people—again, if not used for advertising, or if the people are not made to appear ridiculous.

privacy, obscenity, and libel

Three areas of law apply to the publication of photographs: right-of-privacy, obscenity, and libel. Physical scientists, engineers, mathematicians, and others dealing primarily with things rather than people will rarely be concerned with this problem, but if you are writing in the human, medical, or social sciences, you should protect yourself from lawsuits in advance of publication. Generally, if a photograph or the use made of it does not hold a living person up to ridicule, is not clearly libelous, or is not used for advertising, you should encounter no legal problems. Nevertheless, if a person is recognizable in your photograph and the topic you are dealing with is at all sensitive (for example, medicine, sex, social conditions), it is wise to obtain model releases (see the sample on page 47). If the subject of your photograph has died, try to obtain written permission from next of kin. Although the right to sue is personal, such releases may prevent relatives from taking annoying legal action.

If you have bought photographs from a professional photographer, it is his responsibility to obtain such releases, but you should not knowingly publish unreleased photographs that might be considered illegal invasions of privacy, or are libelous. In any event, although the law protects your right to publish photographs for informative purposes, if you have recognizable people in your photographs, you should learn about the law to protect yourself.

copyright

Copyright laws apply to all works of art such as articles, books, motion pictures, and still photographs. Therefore you cannot publish a copy of a photo without permission of the copyright owner.

Beginning Jan. 1, 1978, all photos become copyright upon creation, whether or not the photographer actually registers the copyright. In fact, a great many photos will never be registered, for the small copyright fee looms large when the number of photos runs into the hundreds. However, under the old copyright law (before Jan. 1, 1978) common law often protects non-copyright photos, and under the new law the photographer owns copyright whether or not it has been registered. (There is some risk in failure to register, but the risk is to the owner, and it does not benefit any would-be copier.)

If the photo you wish to use was made under the old

MODEL RELEASE

I hereby consent to your use, or the use by anyone you authorize, of my name and/or portrait, picture, or photograph of me, for the purpose of illustration and publication.

____

____

date

____

place

MODEL RELEASE
(for minors)

I, the parent/guardian of ____________________________, hereby consent to the use of each of the photographs taken of him/her by ____________________________ or whomever _____ authorizes for purposes of illustration or publication in any manner.

____

parent/guardian

____

date and place

copyright law, it may now be in the public domain, especially if its latest publication was more than 56 years ago. However, there are exceptions, and copying will never be completely safe until 50 years after the death of the photographer.

It is safest—and in the long run simplest—to find in every case who owns copyright and then obtain permission in writing.

You may wish to use old illustrations—those that are in the public domain or old ones for which you have permission. Generally, halftone illustrations are hard to use, as the halftoning process, when used twice or more in succession, yields poor results. Many other kinds of printed illustrations, however, such as steel engravings, woodcuts, and scratchboard drawings, may be reproduced with excellent effect.

credits

Whatever your source of illustrations, you should give proper credit, whether or not you have purchased the photograph, unless you are the photographer. For some copyrighted illustrations, you must cite both the photographer and the copyright owner or publisher. Credits can be placed near the photograph, with the caption, or in a group somewhere in the book, such as on an "acknowledgments" page in the front matter. Whatever method is chosen (generally by the designer), the author must provide complete and accurate information. The photographer's name (correctly spelled) and the copyright owner, if any, must be included; the date that the photograph was taken is helpful. A statement such as "Photo by Dan Tooker" is adequate for privately owned photographs; "Photo by Dan Tooker, courtesy William Kaufmann, Inc., copyright 1976" or "Photo by Dan Tooker, by permission of William Kaufmann, Inc. from *Fiction!* copyright 1976" is suitable wording for previously published photographs, unless the copyright owner specifies otherwise. You may not be told the photographer's name if you are given an institutional photograph. In that case, "Photo courtesy U.S. Department of Agriculture" is adequate credit; again, unless you are told otherwise.

prints

Unless your publisher agrees that you can use color transparencies, you will probably submit photographic prints for illustrations. These should be about 8 inches by 10 inches (20 cm by 25 cm), although some publishers will accept 5-inch by 7-inch (13 cm by 18 cm) or smaller prints. Larger sizes, required for exhibit, can be used, certainly, but they are awkward to handle. Students preparing theses and dissertations may wish to print their photographs on 8½ by 11 inch (22 by 28 cm) thinner paper so that they can be bound more easily. That size and weight of photographic paper must usually be specially ordered, but it is available. Prints should have a good tonal range and be in the sharpest possible focus, as the printing process tends to reduce both brightness and clarity.

publisher's requirements

Most publishers request "glossy" prints, meaning photographs that have been ferrotyped. The reason is that the glossy, ferrotyped surface will retain detail well; in science presentations, detail is usually of primary importance. Resin-coated papers, which provide a glossy surface without troublesome ferrotyping, are welcomed by most printers. Editors may find them difficult to mark on, but the intractable surface may remind you not to damage the print by writing on the back or front of it!

Consult your editor and publisher before submitting prints of color photographs. They may need the negative, or ask you to provide a particular paper surface or use a special photographic printing technique (as, for example, the dye-transfer process).

Once the photographs have been prepared, they should be handled carefully so that the printer will receive them in perfect condition. Each should be properly identified. One good way to do this is to place each photograph in a transparent plastic envelope so that you and your editor and publisher can handle it freely without damaging it. One kind of plastic envelope, available at stationery stores, has three holes punched in a sheet, folded to 8½ by 11 inches (22 by 28 cm). An 8 by 10 inch (20 by 25 cm) photographic print will fit neatly in the envelope, allowing the entire illustration, plastic cover included, to be filed in a notebook or cabinet.

Some publishers request that all photographs be mounted; others request that none be mounted. If your publisher asks for mounted prints, have them dry mounted on stiff cardboard. Dry mounting uses paper that becomes adhesive on heating in a press; when a piece of dry-mount tissue is heated between cardboard and photograph, the board and print are welded together. Many colleges and art schools have dry-mounting presses; so do commercial art stores, who frequently will mount photographs for their customers or allow them to use the store's equipment. Only with great care can rubber cement, an old standby, be applied without developing wrinkles; even if it is well applied, it tends to lose its adhesiveness with age, allowing the photograph to come loose from the backing.

Besides protecting your photographs, you will need to identify them. Here you must exercise utmost caution, for all your effort in obtaining the photographs will be wasted if you damage them while preparing them for the printer. Above all, do not fold, spindle, or mutilate! Do not attack the print with pencil or pen, staple or paper clip. Pens make permanent marks; pencils, staples, and paper clips dent, scratch, and destroy.

It's best not to write on the back of a photograph at all—not with pen, pencil, or crayon—but you must identify it. Probably the best solution is to type all identifying information, including the figure number and caption, on a self-adhesive sticker. Such stickers will adhere to the back of prints of all sorts. It is also wise to have your name and address attached to the illustrations (as well as to the text), and a small address label will do the least damage. Remember to indicate which direction is "up" if needed (see Figure 6).

Some publishers will accept a minimum amount of information pasted or written on each photograph, preferring to have the remaining data (caption, credit, date, your name, title of article) on a separate sheet of paper, keyed to the photographs by the figure number; others wish to have

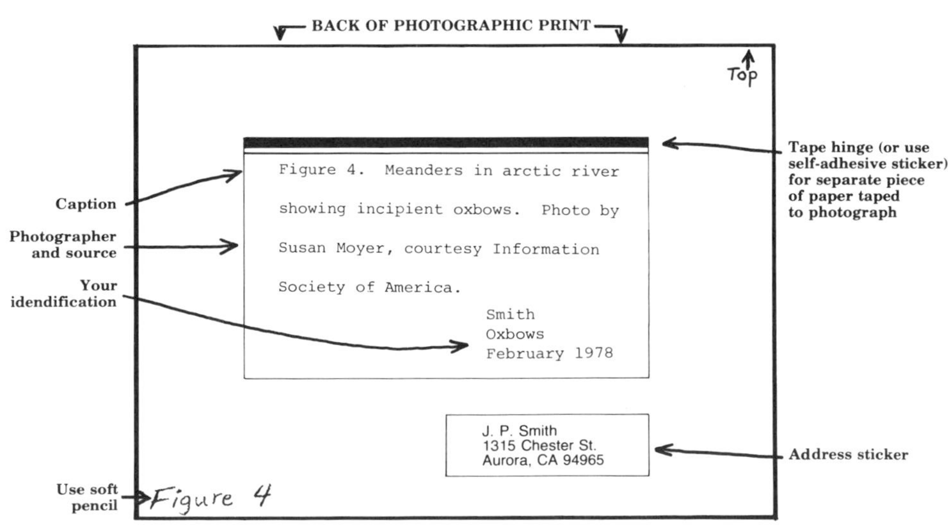

FIGURE 6 One method of marking captions on photographs.

the caption taped to the back of each photograph so that if figure numbers are changed, captions and photographs are not mixed. In any event, you should prepare two copies of the caption, one to be attached to the photograph (either on the back of it or in the same plastic envelope) and one in a list that includes all captions.

cropping

If you can, crop each photograph—that is, eliminate unwanted areas—as you would like to have it when you make your enlargement. If the enlargement does not present the subject exactly as you would like it, you can indicate further cropping to the editor by making a paper mask for the photo. This will not interfere with whatever system your publisher uses for giving instructions to the printer, and it will not damage the photograph. Remember that all photographs do not have to be the same shape; you can crop them into rectangles or squares, if you like. However, you should crop along straight lines and at right angles, unless you are doing special art work.

Here are some suggestions for cropping photographs:

1. Enhance the subject. Crop the photo to stress its purpose. If the caption reads "the rock is horizontally layered," then the best cropping, other factors being equal, would be horizontal.
2. Crop tightly to the subject, maintaining good composition and photographic interest.
3. Crop to improve composition. Reduce distractive elements. focus on the subject, improve balance and relationship of design elements in the photograph.
4. Crop to remove photographic blemishes.
5. Watch the scale. A natural graphic scale is by far the best; if one is indicated by an object in the photograph, don't crop out that object unless you indicate the scale in some other manner.
6. Do not crop people out of a photo if they contribute to viewer interest in the subject or if they indicate scale or depth of field. But do not allow people to distract from the real purpose of the photograph.

retouching

Should you retouch? By all means, if it will improve the photograph. For example: a long panorama may be made from two or more adjoining photographs so neatly that the untrained eye does not discern the join. To do this, prints to be used should be horizontally level and matched for density. If natural junctions are chosen for cut lines (not the square edge of the photographic prints), and the joins are retouched in any obvious place by air brush or some other means, the result will appear to be one continuous photograph. Retouching, then, to improve your presentation—to simplify, to remove blemishes, to concentrate on the subject—is not taboo, so long as you do not distort scientific fact.

over-printing

Don't write on the face of a photograph, even if you would like lettering to appear on the printed picture. One reason is that your lettering would be screened or "half-toned" with the photograph.

If you intend to identify objects in the photograph, draw or letter on a transparent plastic overlay, clearly marked in such a way as to assure proper registration—that is, so that the information on the overlay will be printed exactly where you want it to be printed. Small circles with crosses in them, ⊕, are used for registration. Art-supply stores stock them in adhesive rolls and sheets. Place them outside the margins of both the photograph and the overlay, each circle and cross on the overlay aligned directly over one on the photograph. Three registration marks on each sheet should guarantee registration. Place them outside the boundaries of the photograph so that they will not show on the printed picture.

Art stores also stock letters and numerals in a variety of sizes and styles, as well as symbols and patterns, suitable for doing professional lettering on your overlays.

Once you have made an overlay, treat it, too, with care. Remember that any writing you do, even erased pencil marks drawn for guidance, or words you have written on a sheet of paper on top of the photograph or overlay, may be invisible to the unaided eye, and yet leave pressure marks that will show when printed.

captions

You can prepare three main kinds of captions for photographs, but generally you should not mix them. One kind is a caption that reinforces the text—repeats, probably in different words, the same information that the text includes. New matter in such a caption is confined to details of the photograph: when and where it was taken and who the photographer was. Another kind presents information not included in the text. The third kind gives only the figure number or other identification (perhaps only an arrow), leaving the text to convey all verbal information. Whichever kind you choose (perhaps in consultation with your publisher), you should use it throughout your book or paper. Even if you choose the third kind of caption, you must provide your publisher with proper crediting information (photographer, source of photograph or permission, date) and, if needed, scale.

Don't be afraid that your publisher will think you egotistical if your name appears on every piece of paper and bit of art work that you submit. "Fool's names" does not apply here; he'll think you wise, not foolish.

digging deeper

An excellent book on the legal problems of photography is *Photography and the Law,* by George Chernoff and Hershel Sarbin (1971;Amphoto, New York). Both men are lawyers; one is the publisher of an American photographic magazine, the other is a legal counsel for professional photographers and photographic societies. They distinguish between the right to take photographs and the right to publish them, and discuss the laws of U.S. copyright and libel.

Books on composition in art abound, although the subject of photographic composition is not necessarily dealt with. In the small book called *Photography* by Wyatt B. Brummitt, R. Will Burnett, and Herbert S. Zim (1971; Golden Press, New York;), several pages deal with photographic composition specifically, and much of the book contains information on composition. *The Art of Photography* in the Life Library of Photography (1971; Time-Life Books, New York) has a well-illustrated, clearly presented chapter entitled "The Principles of Design."

Now: suppose you need an illustration and hope that somewhere there is something to meet your need. In that case try *The Picture Researcher's Handbook* (Hilary and Mary Evans and Andra Nelki, 1974; Charles Scribner's Sons, New York). The subtitle is *An International Guide to Picture Sources—and How to Use Them.* The book includes an introduction to searching, a directory of sources, and four indexes.

A somewhat similar work is *Picture Sources 3: Collections of Prints and Photographs in the U.S. and Canada* (edited by Ann Novotny and Rosemary Eakins, 1975; Special Libraries Association, New York).

key points

In selecting and handling photographs:

- obtain the best possible photographs of your subject
- get releases from subjects and from copyright owners
- credit photographers and sources
- handle and label photographs with care
- write informative captions

11 DRAWING: preparing drawings and diagrams

technical illustration

Drawings and diagrams for publication can be made in two ways, one depending upon mathematical techniques (mechanical drafting) and one upon artistic skill. Mechanical drafting is what is generally known as technical illustration, although that term is also sometimes used for artistic renditions of technical subjects. By using mechanical drawing techniques, a skilled draftsman can produce three-dimensional drawings, true to scale, that show objects from various points of view. Architect's plans, electrical, electronic, aeronautical, and mechanical layouts, ship designs—all these, and many of their relatives (most of which are so accurately drawn that they are truly maps) are technical illustrations drawn by people experienced in mechanical drafting.

engineering drawings

Engineering drawings of this sort, and similar drawings and diagrams, can be used for illustrations if the lettering and lines will be legible when reduced to printed size. Convention in this kind of drawing allows for many bordering lines and boxes, filled with lettering, as well as identification letters and symbols that have meaning only within the organization where they originated. All this material becomes clutter when published. You would be wise to simplify any engineering drawing you use by eliminating much of the bordering material. If such material is necessary to the understanding of the drawing, include it in the caption; if not, leave it out. Many engineering drawings have spaces designated for executive approval, which obviously can be removed for publication.

Such drawings as these are made to serve as plans from which an object can be built. For that reason, scale and precision are critical. Diagrams that show how things that already exist operate do not need to be drawn with such exactness; they can be diagrams, rather than maps. Such drawings, in which scale is of little or no importance, include "how to" diagrams, flow sheets, and organizational charts.

exploded views

A kind of illustration halfway between photograph and drawing is the exploded view, which shows an object separated into its parts in such a way that one can see clearly how the parts fit together. This can be made from a photograph, which may be cut apart and air brushed, or from a drawing. Parts are identified by "call-outs"—leaders (lines) running from the illustration of the part to the name of the part or to information about its function (see Figure 7).

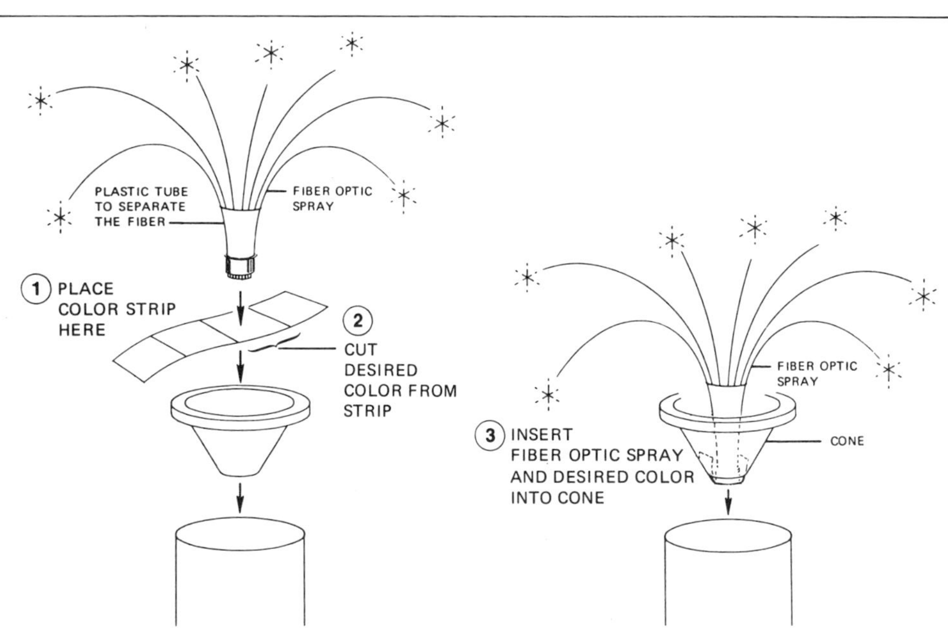

FIGURE 7 Exploded view (this one a drawing, not a photograph) of a fiber optics lamp showing how its parts fit together.

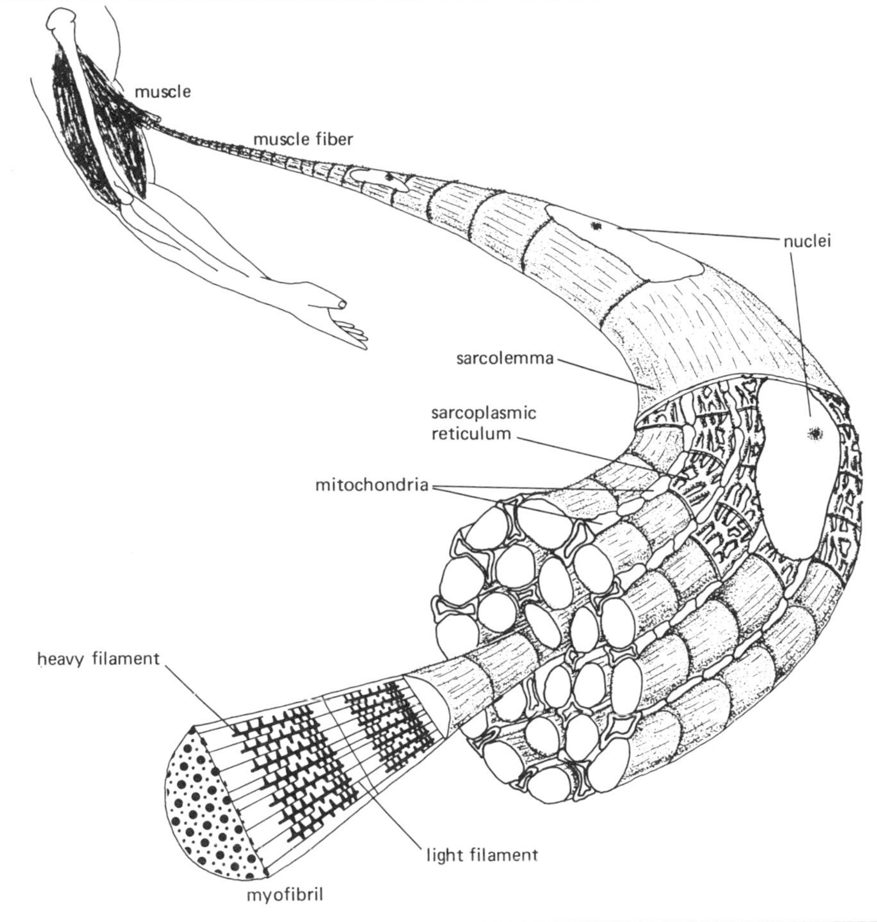

Expanded view of the structure of a striated muscle. Here, the artist has not separated the various parts, but has enlarged them, so that the viewer is led from a sketch of an arm to a microscopic view of its composition. FIGURE 8

machine-made drawings

Drawings made entirely by machine are also used for technical illustration. Some can be made by computer (including maps); others are simply the records produced by the machines themselves. Among the host of machine records used are oscilloscope records, electrocardiograms, differential thermal analysis records, seismograms, and sub-bottom profiles. Not all can be used without redrawing, as they may be too complex to make clear illustrations, or may have colored grids or colored lines. Remember that brown, red, yellow, and orange will reproduce as black; green becomes gray, and light blue will not show at all.

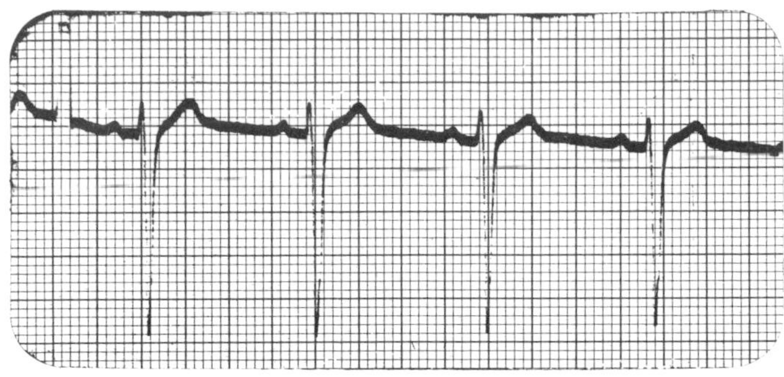

FIGURE 9. Part of an electrocardiogram as recorded from a patient. The grid shown here allows the physician to read the graph directly. However, you may need to rework a graph such as this to use it as an illustration, as the grid may be too obtrusive, or the tracing too faint, or it may require border material for explanation.

woodcuts and metal plates

The earliest form of book illustration was the woodcut, which dates back about as far as movable type. Reproductions using wood are made in two ways: wood block, the older method, is a form of relief printing, by which areas not to be printed are cut out. It was modified into wood engraving, an intaglio process, by which the line to be printed was incised. An enormous number of prints can be made by wood engraving—over 900,000 copies are said to have been made from one of Thomas Bewick's newspaper illustrations. Although other artists experimented with the technique, Bewick's contribution was to use the more durable end grain of the wood with such success that he is often called the developer of the wood block.

Forms of intaglio printing—principally etching and engraving—using metal plates (copper, zinc, and steel) replaced wood as the principal method of book illustration until colloidal gel processes and modern halftoning methods were developed (see page 129).

All these methods, relief and intaglio, as well as such other similar techniques as collage and silk-screen printing, are still used by graphic artists (Figure 10). However, as an artist must go through several stages to obtain prints by any of these graphic methods (he must draw, etch or engrave, and print), it is unlikely that you would ask that such illustrations be made. You may, however, wish to use illustrations of this kind that have already been published. If they are out of copyright, you need only to obtain a good photograph of them. If they are in color (as, for example, the splendid ukiyo-e Japanese wood block prints), you can photograph them in color, but they must then be printed as if they were color photographs.

It is possible, of course, that you may wish to commission an entire book to be illustrated by one of these methods. The results can be very handsome, as, for example, Pablo Picasso's 20th century aquatint illustrations (a form of intaglio printing using resin) for Comte de Buffon's 18th century *Histoire Naturelle*. The expense, however, can be great.

FIGURE 10

Print of coast redwood, *Sequoia sempervirens,* made by inking the leaves and stem of the plant, then pressing it onto absorbent paper. "Plant prints" are among a host of different forms of graphic materials than can serve as illustrations if presented in a clear, uncluttered, professional manner.

pen and ink It is far more likely that you will require or prefer drawings. Pen-and-ink sketches (Figure 11) are the most commonly used for scientific purposes, although pencil sketches, wash drawings, scratchboard, and others may also be helpful. Certain kinds of drawings to be used for diagnostic purposes (fossil identification, archaeological description, anatomical detail, for example) have rigid requirements; drawings to be used for more general purposes have wider latitude. For pencil and other forms of rendering that smear in handling, ask your artist to cover the drawing with a fixative spray.

working with your artist Discuss your needs thoroughly with the artist before he (or she) begins your work. Make certain that he understands its purpose, what the format is to be, how much his product will be reduced, and whether or not he can use

FIGURE 11 Pen-and-ink sketch of underseascape of Paleozoic time (350 million years ago). Although the animals shown here are drawn as nearly as possible to "life," using fossil remains as models, the entire scene is, of course, imaginary. Except to photograph a scale model, an artist's rendition is the only way to recreate the geologic past graphically.

color. If color is to be used, determine with him whether he will produce the separations himself in the form of overlays, or whether he will do one illustration in color that will later require photographic separation. Although the second method is easier for the artist, it is more expensive to print.

If you do have fine drawings made that you would like to keep (suppose you had commissioned Picasso's aquatints, for example), have an understanding with your publisher and printer that they are to be returned undamaged. Printers have a reputation among artists (deserved or not) of having a high regard for only their own work. After they have made a negative and plate, they may treat the original with very little care, as its main purpose, in their eyes, has been served. Many times, this is of no consequence; but if the original art work has been returned with footprints, smudges, or ink spots, or has been folded, you or your artist may be very much upset.

digging deeper

The literature on drawings and diagrams is vast, although textbooks and articles on the techniques of mechanical drawing are far fewer than books on art. Nevertheless, any good engineering library can provide a selection of books on technical illustration. Two recent books have that title: *Technical Illustration.* One is by T.A. Thomas (1968; McGraw Hill); the other by J.C. Gibby (1970; American Technical Society, Chicago).

Books on art, ranging from 16-page "how to" pamphlets to monographs on aesthetics, drawing, painting, sketching, printmaking, and other forms of art abound. It is not likely that you will undertake to do your own drawing; if you are qualified to make professional sketches, you do not need our advice on how to do it!

What you will need to know in order to advise your artist properly is what size and shape to make the drawings, and what printing method will be used to reproduce them. All of this you will need to find out from your publisher; however, you will be able to guide your artist better if you and he both have an understanding of printing techniques. Pages 128-130 and the references on page 131 will help you.

key points

Before making drawings, plan

- purpose
- format
- reduction

Make drawings

- simple
- clear
- precise

12
CHARTING: making graphs and charts

Graphs are drawings that replace numbers. They give a quick, clear picture of numerical information—information that could also be shown on a table. Graphs are like slide rules: they give very fast information, but are not completely accurate. If you want to give your readers an immediate mental picture, make a graph; if you wish them to know all details, make a table.

Graphs have advantages over tables in that they allow readers to interpolate between points and to make predictions. Graphs can be used for forecasting because they show trends—a fact that anyone who has watched the stock market will appreciate.

the basic form

The basic form of the graph is a cross—a horizontal line (the X axis, or abscissa) perpendicular to a vertical line (the Y axis, or ordinate). These two coordinates (the ordinate and the abscissa) define the units measured—in graphs, two or more variables are shown. Positive values are plotted toward the top and right; negative values are plotted to the bottom and left. As you can see in Figure 12, the four quadrants defined are numbered counterclockwise.

Scientists and engineers often need to refer to both positive and negative values on a graph; others generally need only quadrant I, where all values are positive. In this quadrant, the horizontal scale is shown along the base, and the vertical scale is on the left.

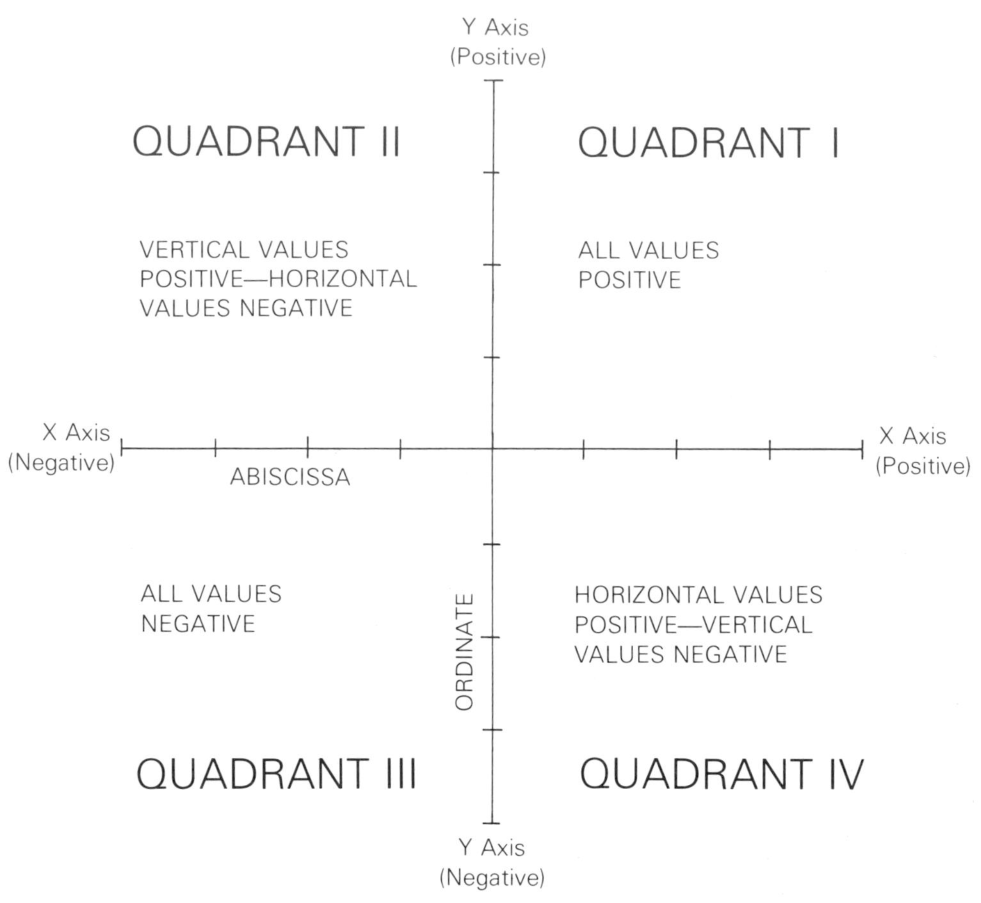

FIGURE 12 Basic framework for charts and graphs.

scales Within the quadrant you can plot your information, later connecting the points, if you wish, with a line. You can use any scale or division of units that you like, but Figure 13 shows how a change of scale affects the appearance of a line. Although the information plotted is the same, the impression given the reader is quite different for each. Remember that all graphs do not need to use zero as a base, but if an entire scale is not shown, you should make a slight visual break to alert your readers to the gap.

curves A graph can show more than one curve: sometimes a comparison of curves, or the relationship of one to another is the principal feature of the graph. Figure 14 shows several variables on one graph. Make certain, however, that

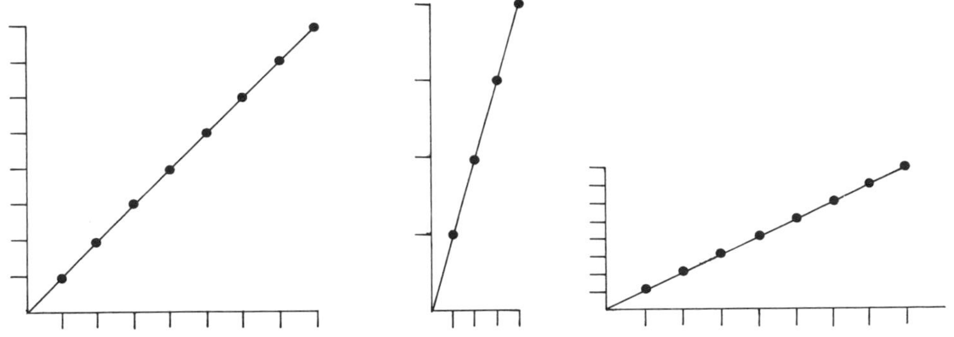

FIGURE 13

How altering the vertical or horizontal scale on a graph changes the visual appearance of a plotted line. In the graph to the left, vertical and horizontal measurements are at the same scale; in center, the vertical scale has been extended, the horizontal compressed; right, the horizontal chart is the same as at the left, but the vertical has been condensed. The values plotted were the same for each graph.

you do not have so many variables on the graph that it becomes a discouraging forest of lines. Bear in mind that graphs are meant to improve clarity. To make it easier for readers to understand your graph, you can make "tick" marks that will help them to judge the two values of the curve at any point. Be careful not to overpower the graph with too many such marks.

lines and areas

The line graph can be changed into an area graph by shading or coloring to emphasize quantities, as shown in Figure 15, which is a multiple-surface graph, or area graph. It can be used to compare related categories; a full (100 percent) area graph (see Figure 15) can be used to show relationships of parts to the whole, as well as individual details.

When two or more variables are related to one another, they are, in statistical terminology, as well as logic, "correlated." If both increase or decrease together, they are said to have positive correlation; if one increases as the other decreases, they have negative correlation. Not only the fact of relationship, but also the degree of it and the character of variations, can be shown on correlation charts.

ratio graphs

Engineers and scientists also use ratio graphs, in which one scale is not arithmetic, but logarithmic. (Logarithmic scales are not suitable for area graphs or bar charts.)

Semi-logarithmic, or ratio graphs, usually have one axis ruled arithmetically and the other ruled logarithmically. This allows the condensation of large quantities because the logarithmic scale is a power rather than an arithmetic intercept. Choose a graph paper suitable to your needs: if the largest value in the series is less than ten times the smallest, use one-cycle division; if more, use two- or three-cycle. When your information has been plotted (remember, one axis shows powers—1, 2, 3 for 10, 20, 30, for example—and the other arithmetic divisions—1, 2, 3 for 1, 2, 3), you can show the rate of change of your figures by means of the curve that you plot. A straight ascending line is the form taken by figures increasing at an increasing rate; decreasing at a decreasing rate is shown by a straight descending line. The greater the slope of the line, the

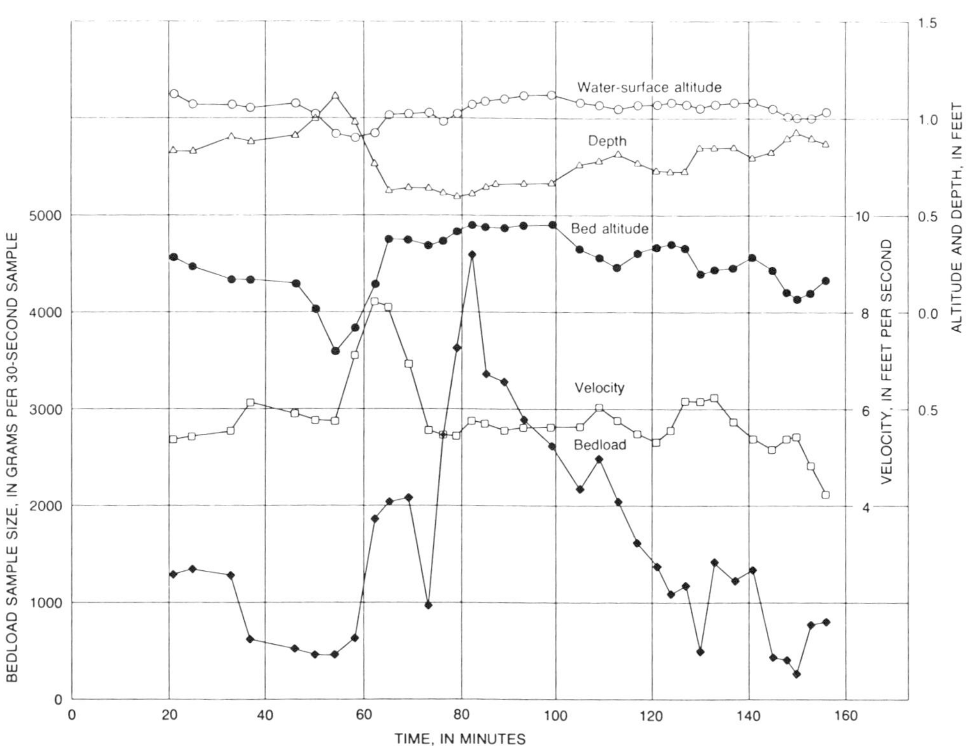

FIGURE 14 Several curves can be combined into one graph, if they can be distinguished from one another. Here, scales on left and right differ. Although this graph is quite clear on a printed page, it would make a disturbing lecture slide.

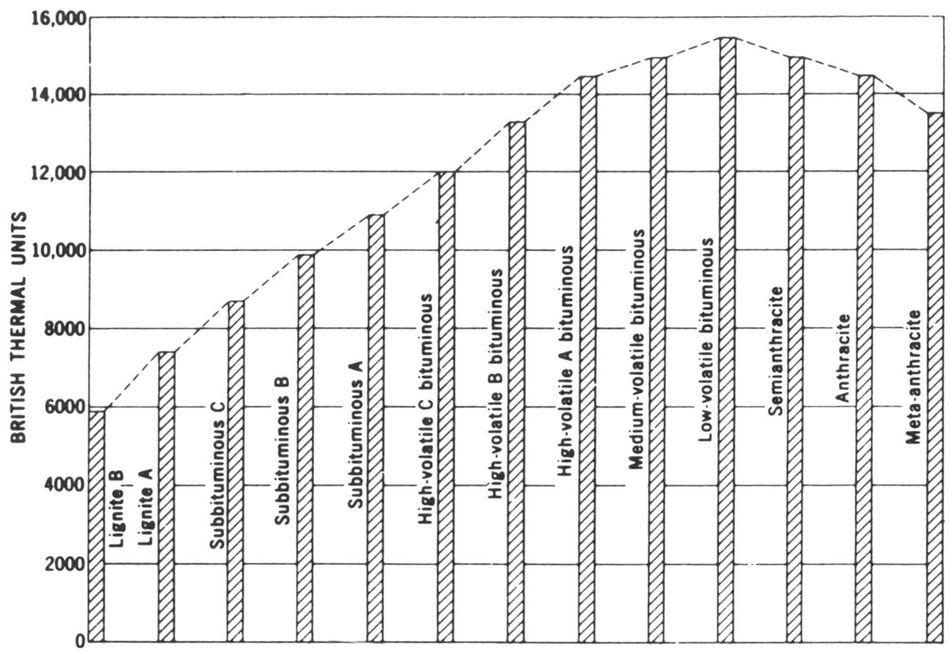

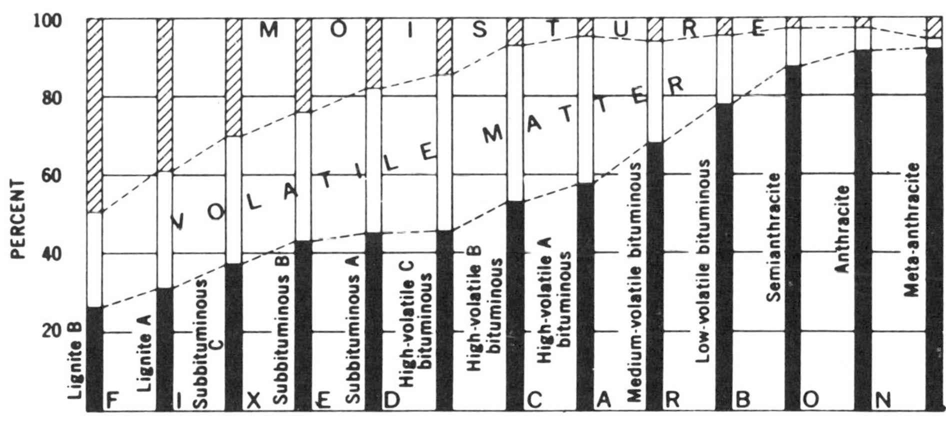

FIGURE 15

Two graphs comparing types of coal. Top, a graph made from a column chart, showing heating value. Bottom, a 100 percent area graph showing the chemical content of the same types of coal. It, too, was made from a column chart.

greater the rate of change. An example is shown in Figure 16.

Take care in interpolating the logarithmic scale of a semi-logarithmic graph and both scales of a logarithmic graph. Remember that powers of numbers, not the numbers themselves, are shown.

If you need to plot three variables, you can make a trilinear (ternary) graph, a special form of area graph (Figure 17).

Unless your audience needs precise information or uses your graphs as tools directly, you may want to change your simple line graphs into pictorial graphs, where your main points will be strengthened by suitable art work. Pictorial graphs are especially useful for emphasizing a few items.

bars and columns

Some charts, as we use the word in this chapter (certain kinds of charts fall into the category of maps) measure only one variable, in contrast to graphs, that measure two or more. Often, that variable is numerical (as in Figure 15, top) or expressed in percentage (15, bottom).

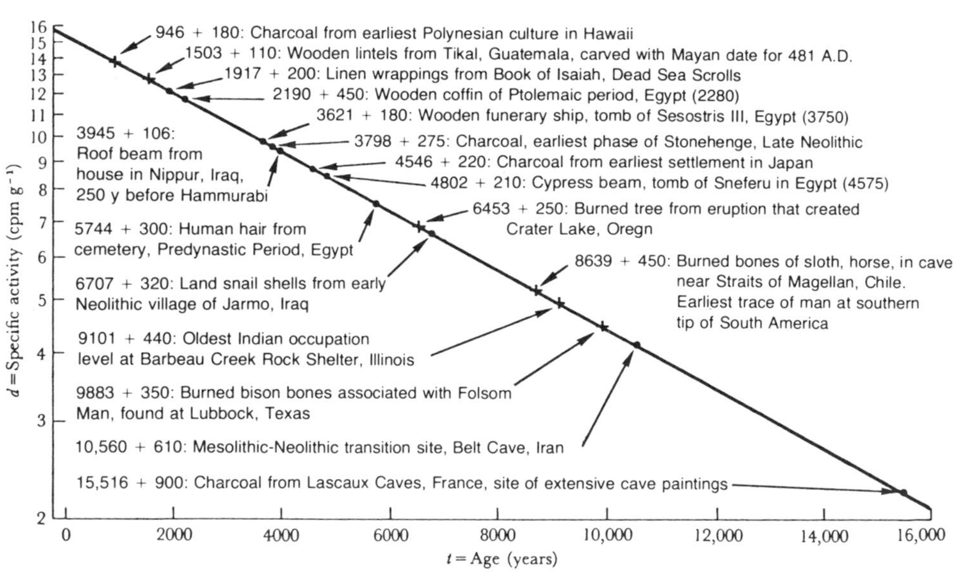

FIGURE 16 A semilogarithmic (or ratio) chart, plotting the decay rate of carbon-14 against the age of the sample in years. Charts like this are valuable to show rates of change, but not absolute change.

Units on the chart may be shown horizontally or vertically. You can change many graphs into bar or column charts, if you think the information will be more telegraphic, or more usable.

You can group information on bar charts, thereby contrasting groups and individual parts of the group, or you can mark the column charts to show percentage units (see Figure 15). Bar or column charts also lend themselves to pictorial techniques.

pies

The percentage "pie" chart is another familiar friend. It is a favorite of those who have control of purse strings, as it can show percentages and money very clearly. Each piece of pie is a part of the whole, so the reader can see easily

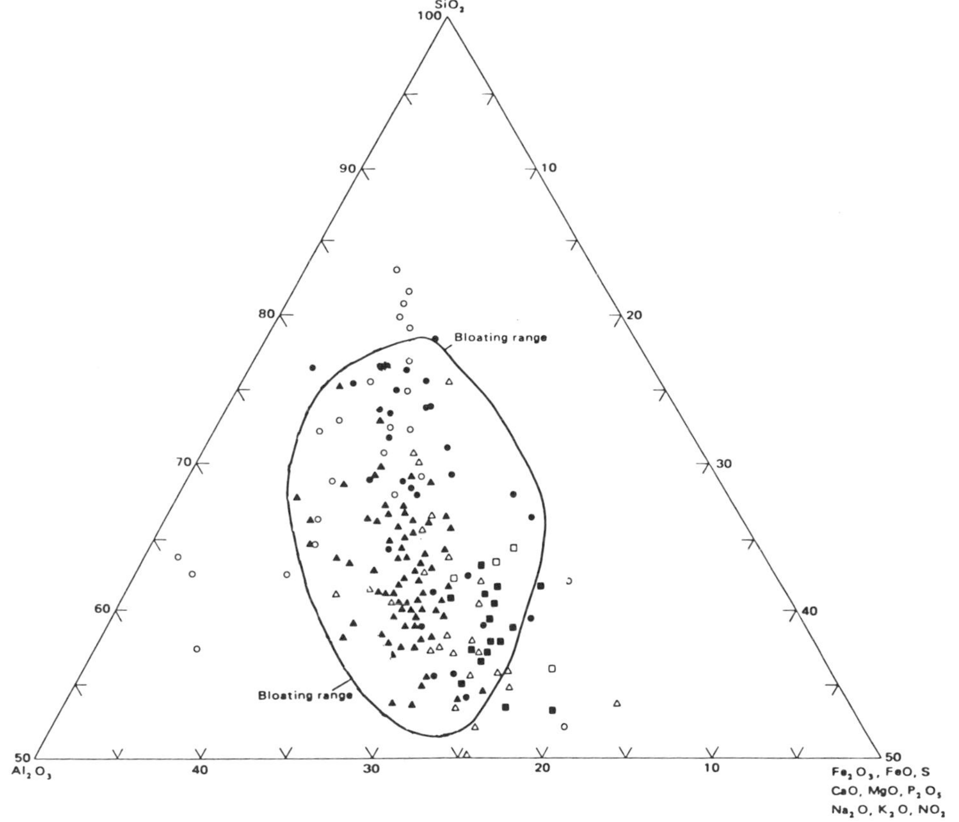

FIGURE 17

Trilinear (ternary) graph showing three variables. Here, chemical constituents of "bloating" shale (solid forms) are compared with non-bloating shale (open forms). Bloating shale expands when heated.

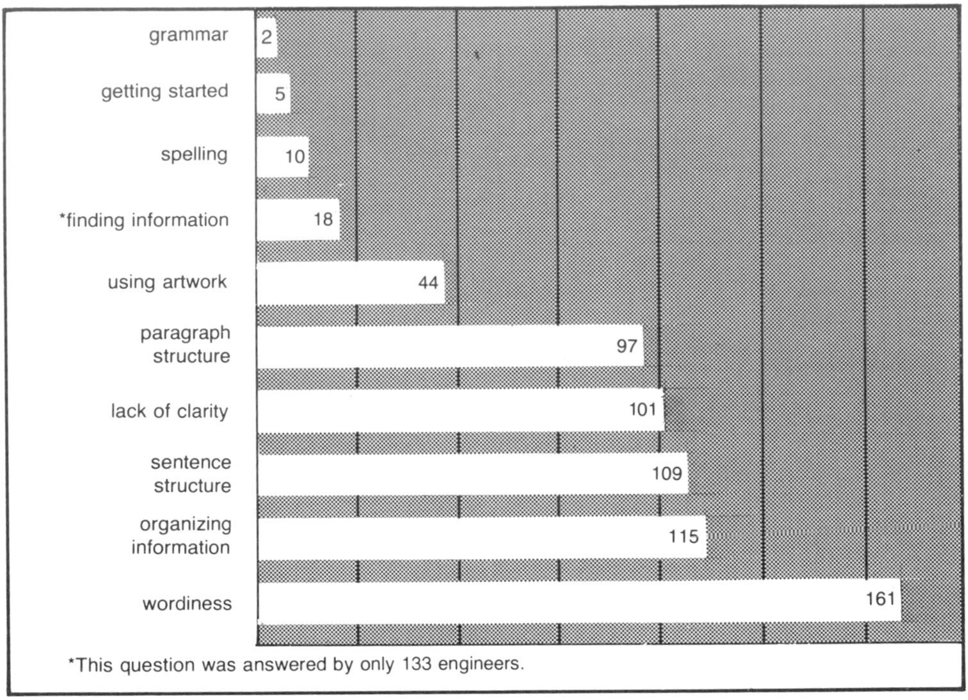

grammar	2
getting started	5
spelling	10
*finding information	18
using artwork	44
paragraph structure	97
lack of clarity	101
sentence structure	109
organizing information	115
wordiness	161

*This question was answered by only 133 engineers.

These Writing Weaknesses Were Recognized by Engineers . . .
. . . Whose Writing Involved Primarily Memos, Reports, and Letters

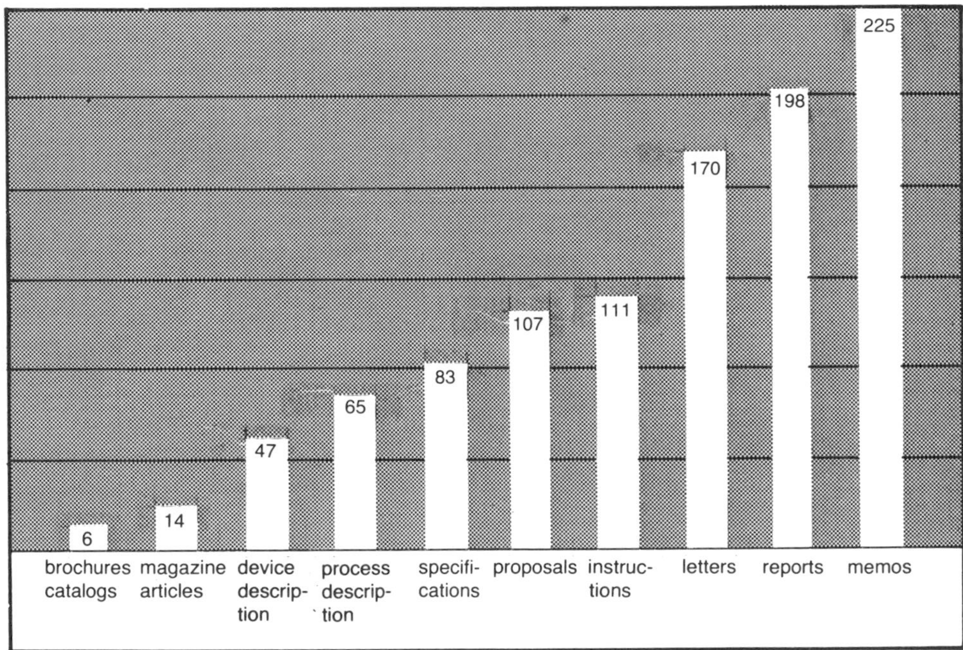

← Bar chart (top) and column chart (below). Here, the actual number of engineers responding to each question is marked on the bar or column. Only five had trouble getting started writing, but 161 could not stop! What this chart does not show is how many engineers were canvassed—at least 225. FIGURE 18

A simple pictorial pie showing percentage as "cents." ↓ FIGURE 19

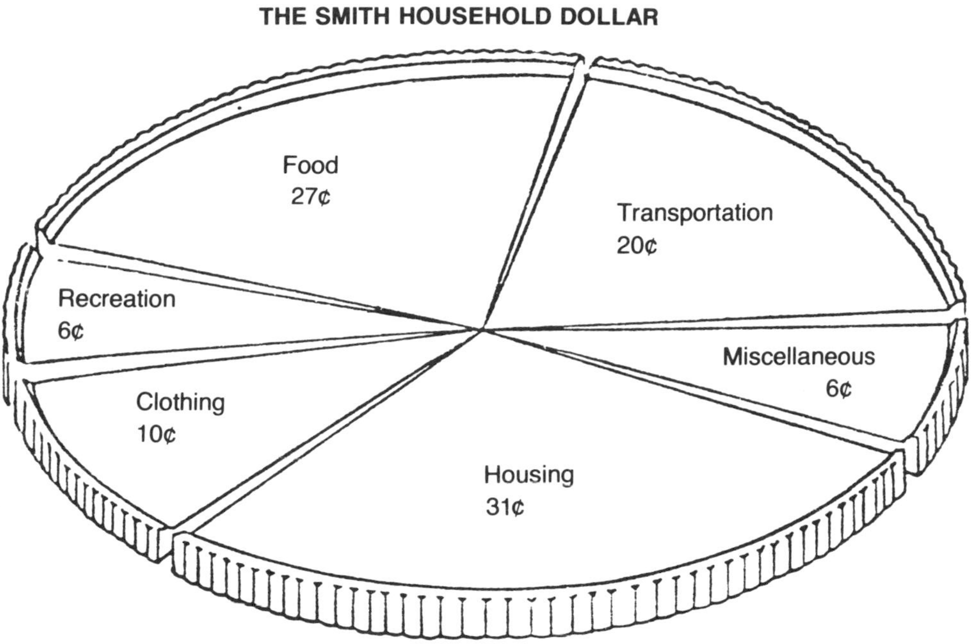

THE SMITH HOUSEHOLD DOLLAR

Food
27¢
Transportation
20¢
Recreation
6¢
Miscellaneous
6¢
Clothing
10¢
Housing
31¢

what fraction each item represents. The pie chart, like the bar chart, lends itself to pictorial representation, particularly as coins are discs and can be drawn as "pies" (Figure 19).

roses

The "rose" is a special form of circular chart that measures percentage and also gives compass directions. It is a column chart, the columns being constructed outward from the center of a circle, each column proportional to its value, and its map direction indicates compass orientation. Like a map, a rose is related to a particular place—the place where the measurements were made.

check-points

When your graph or chart has been completed by the artist, check it carefully to make certain that it tells your readers what you intend it to. Check especially for these points:

1. Are the data plotted correctly? Bear in mind that an error in plotting may be in your artist's rendition,

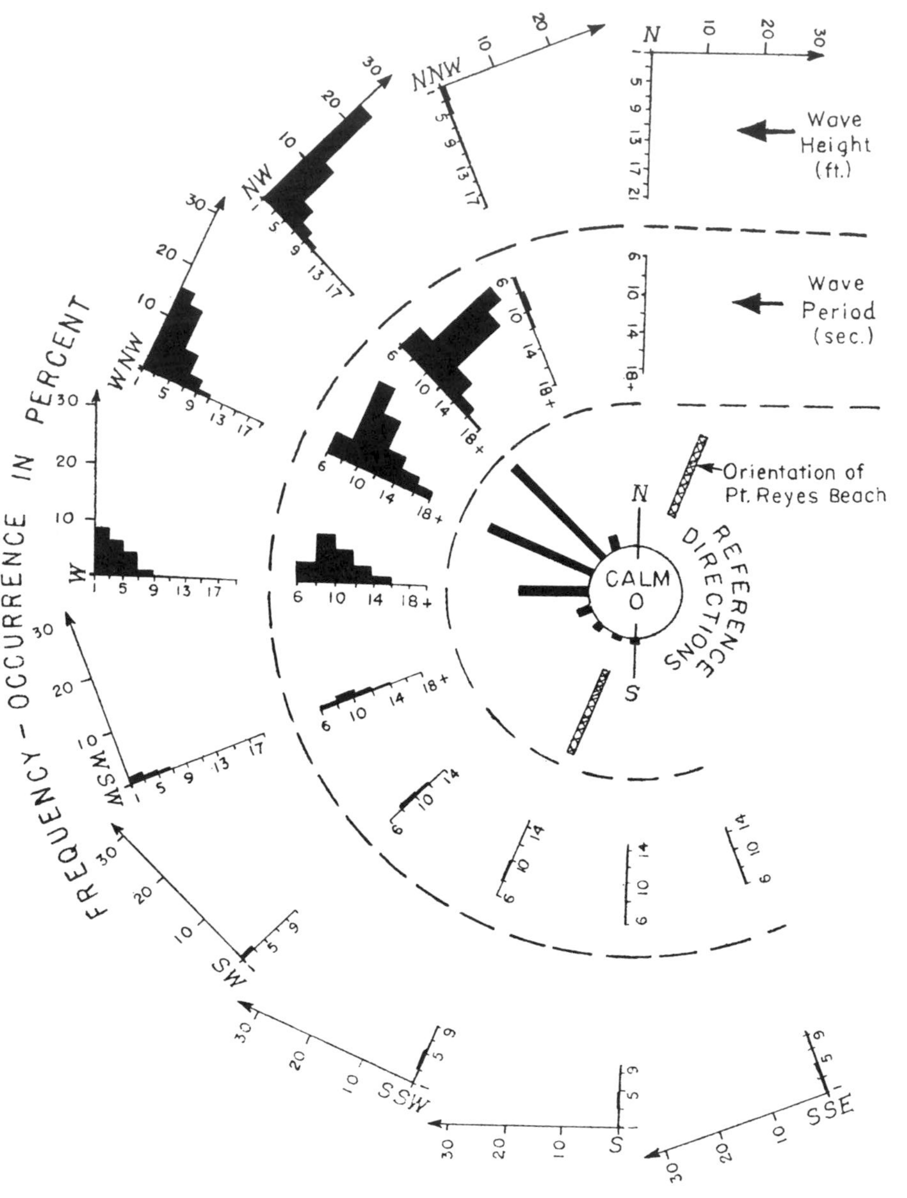

FIGURE 20 Rose showing wave direction, wave period, and wave height at Point Reyes National Seashore, California. Length of bars indicates frequency; direction gives orientation. Much information is condensed graphically in such diagrams.

in his translation of what you wrote, or in your own original plotting.

2. Are all words spelled correctly?
3. Are all numbers correct and correctly plotted?
4. Do symbols in the legend match those on the graph? Are there symbols on the graph not identified on the legend, or symbols in the legend not used on the graph? There should not be!
5. Is the scale correctly given? Does it say "feet" although it should read "meters"? Has the scale of the graph been altered but not the graphic scale?

Whatever form of chart or graph you choose, remember your audience. Be sure that they will understand it, and that you have clarified the subject, not confused it. Remember these rules for all art work (for that matter, for the written word as well):

Be direct.
Be simple.
Be clear.
Be accurate.

digging deeper

Most books on college algebra or statistics tell how to plot and read graphs; textbooks on mechanical drawing or drafting are helpful in construction and design of graphs and charts. *Engineering–Technical Drafting and Graphics,* by J.W. Giachino and Henry J. Beukema (1961; American Technical Society), has a comprehensive and useful chapter on graphs and charts, of particular help to those constructing charts and graphs for a technical audience.

If your audience is not technically oriented, you may find the clear, simple presentations suggested in *Making the Most of Charts, an ABC of Graphic Presentation,* prepared by the American Telephone and Telegraph Company (1960; American Management Association, Bulletin 28) exactly the approach you need. It is, however, just that: an approach to presentation, not detailed instructions.

Graphic Charts Handbook, by Anna C. Rogers (Public Affairs Press, 1961; Washington, D.C.) provides a balance between nontechnical and technical presentations. Comprehensive in its coverage of graphic methods, it gives a wide variety of examples and considerable detail on construction of charts and graphs.

As Rogers points out, the literature of graphic presentation is "incredibly meager." None of the three books cited gives much about the preparation of charts and graphs for publication. *Engineering–Technical Drafting* assumes that you are preparing charts for technical use; *Making the Most of Charts* emphasizes oral presentations; even *Graphic Charts Handbook,* which does deal with reproduction of charts, assumes that the chart will be reproduced independently, and the methods of reproduction described are such forms as photocopying, mimeographing, and blueprinting.

How to Lie with Statistics (Darrell Huff, 1954; Norton, New York) isn't so much about telling you how to mislead your readers as how to keep from deluding yourself. Too little knowledge about statistics is indeed dangerous, and this book will help you tell the truth with numbers, charts, and graphs.

key points

Choose graphs and charts to

- display information
- show comparisons
- show trends
- allow predictions

13
MAPPING:
constructing maps

Maps are diagrams that show how space is organized. The area can be vast or minute, the scale small or large, the objects represented in the space natural or man-made—even imaginary. Andreas Vesalius' anatomical drawings and Nicolaus Copernicus' diagrams of the universe—two landmarks in the history of modern science—are maps, even as are maps of chromosomes, atoms, and crystal structure. In a sense, knitting instructions and indexes are word maps, as they help readers to find their way.

They are not, however, illustrations, as most maps are. Maps, as we commonly think of them, take their reference from the Earth, and although astronomical maps (with scales in light-years) and molecular maps (with scales in micrometers) are legitimate maps, they are special cases that can be treated as diagrams rather than as conventional maps.

reference points

Earth maps take their reference from arbitrary points. Many globes of Earth show lines circling them—some around the poles, parallel to each other (latitude), and others extending from pole to pole (longitude). All of the longitude lines (meridians) are great circles—that is, the maximum distance around the Earth—but of latitude lines, only the equator is a great circle; all others are smaller. All these lines, latitude and longitude, have been given num-

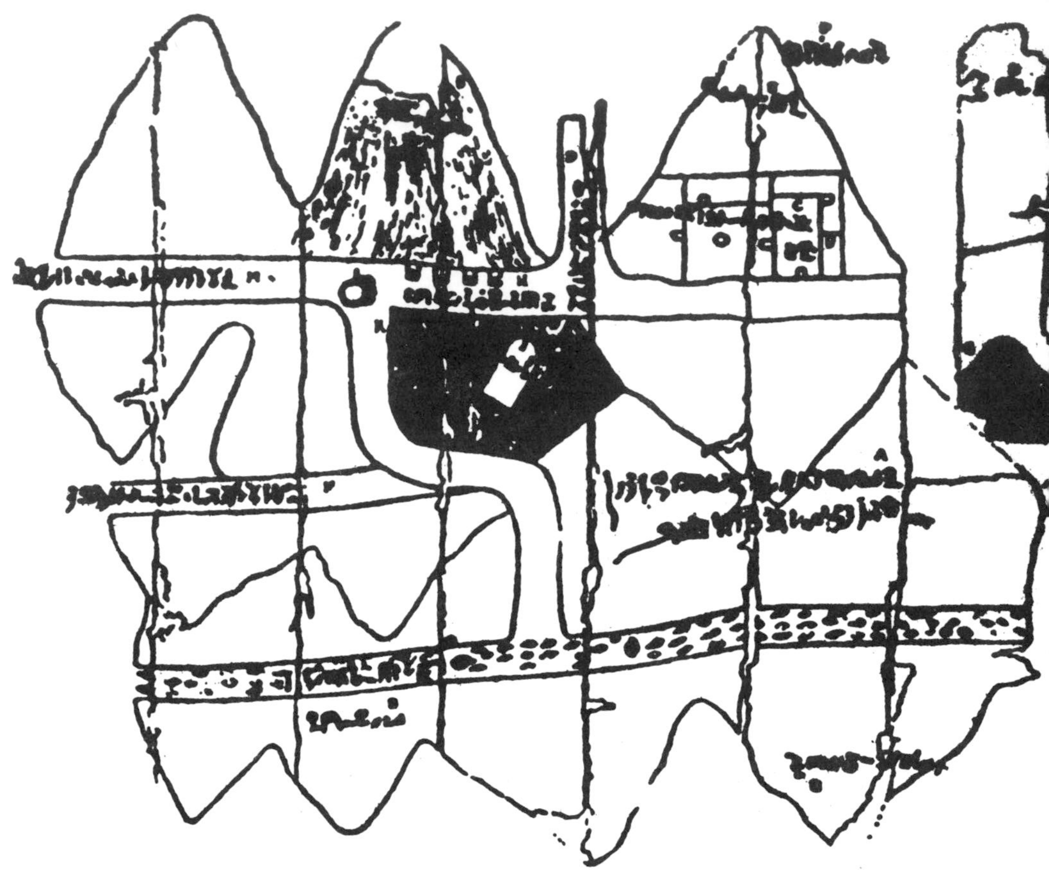

FIGURE 21 An early map, showing the location of gold mines in Egyptian times. Many maps, even today, show land areas with reference to known objects—islands, towns, rocks, even trees—but without reference to latitude, longitude, or any official land grid.

bers, starting from the equator for latitude and from a point in England (Greenwich, the site of an ancient observatory) for longitude. This divides the Earth neatly into segments on a globe. Unfortunately, these lines are arbitrary and imaginary and so they cannot be seen on the Earth itself. Instead, by using magnetic instruments for measuring the Earth, and telescopic instruments for identifying the positions of heavenly bodies, a surveyor or map maker must determine where on Earth he is relative to these imaginary lines.

projections

Once a map maker has determined his location, he (or she) encounters the problem of how to write it down. Maps are printed on two-dimensional pieces of paper, which can never wholly reflect the three-dimensional Earth, nor can they show accurately the curving surface of the globe. Many mechanical and mathematical projections of the rotund Earth onto flat paper have been made, and many more are possible, but all are compromises, and none can show both true area and correct shape. Each shows the

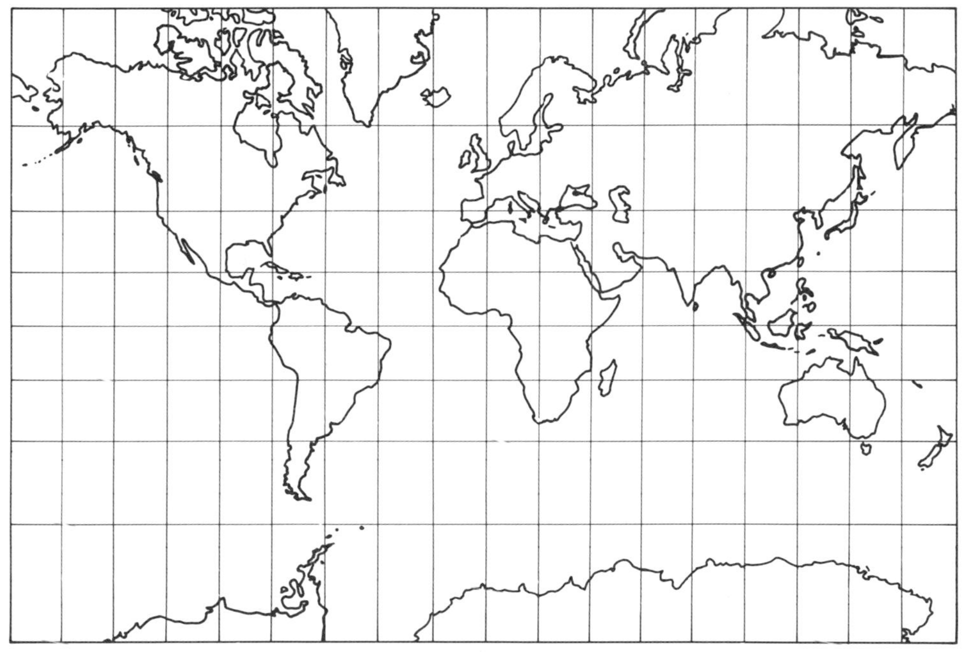

FIGURE 22

Most of the Earth as shown on Mercator's projection. Mercator, who first used the word "atlas" to describe a collection of maps, published the first part of his famous atlas in 1585. (Atlas was a mythological personage who bore the heavens on his shoulders.) On Mercator's projection, parallels of latitude are spaced correctly to scale, while longitude lines are straight. This makes a convenient map for navigation, but distorts land areas, particularly near the poles.

All parallels of latitude are the same length as the equator; this is not true on the globe itself, where only the equator is a great circle. For that reason, the user must realize that the scale of the map changes from place to place. Inconvenient for many purposes, the projection has the great advantage of constant bearings, thereby making it easy to plot a sailing course. (Maps for sailing and air navigation are often called "charts," but these are not similar to the "charts" described on pages 63-74.)

The national maps of Great Britain, Australia, Canada, Italy, Norway, and New Zealand, as well as maps of the United States made by the U.S. Army, use a special form of the Mercator projection called the Transverse Mercator projection.

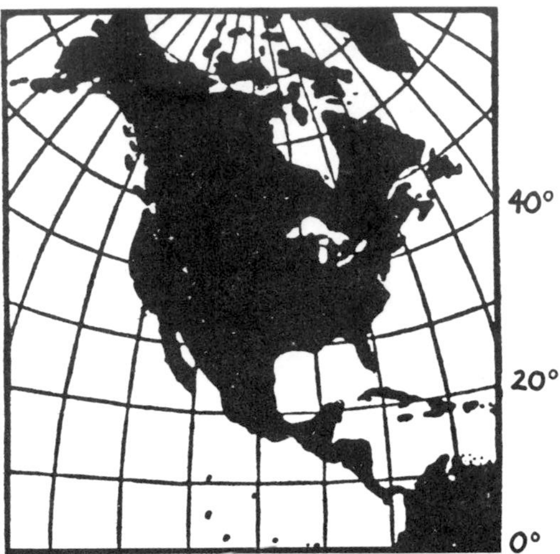

FIGURE 23 Polyconic projections, upon which the topographic maps of the U.S. are based, show land shape of small areas more accurately than the Mercator, as the radius for each parallel of latitude is plotted correctly. This type of projection allows the fitting together of many sheets.

Earth slightly differently; land areas assume different outlines depending upon the type of projection. All older sea maps and many modern ones use a Mercator projection, devised by Gerhardus Mercator, a 16th century geographer (see Figure 22). Many of our current official land maps use a polyconic projection (see Figure 23).

To make a map by surveying the land itself, one must start from known points, usually "benchmarks"—already established as points in a cadastral net by government surveyors, or from some other surveyed point. It is possible, of course, to make maps that refer only to landmarks, not to an established surveyed base. In New England, for example, early surveying was done by "metes and bounds" which used mountains, trees, roads, and fences for markers, all of which (even mountains) are changeable or mortal. For that reason, modern maps are tied to an arbitrary, albeit imaginary, land net that refers to longitude and latitude.

permissions

Probably you will not be constructing a map from the ground up as an illustration for your publication. Most authors use some already existing map as a base, adding to and deleting from it for their own use. Here, take heed:

many maps are copyrighted. You cannot copy them or rework them without permission of the copyright owner. In particular, beware of maps in atlases published by private firms and of maps sold by oil companies for use by motorists. They are thoroughly copyrighted. Sometimes a map publisher will introduce unusual marks or minute errors on maps so that they can identify unauthorized use. If you intend to use a copyrighted map, ask permission of the owner, and do not be surprised if payment is requested.

You can use most maps published by various government agencies without concern for copyright. Sources of such maps are given at the end of this chapter.

common scales

In the United States, the federal government has been making maps throughout its history. Many maps are available from the government. For land areas, the fundamental maps are topographic quadrangles, currently issued in scales ranging from 1:24,000 (1 inch equals 2,000 feet) to 1,250,000 (1 inch equals about 4 miles) (see table, page 81). For coastal areas, the basic maps are nautical charts, which are on larger scales. Topographic maps show land elevations, cities, roads, lakes, rivers, and other features visible on land; nautical charts show water depths, hazards and aids to navigation, bottom details, and the like. Maps issued especially for pilots show both land and sea, but emphasize landmarks and air hazards. The U.S. government has issued charts of this kind on fairly large scale for most of the world.

accuracy standards

In order to insure that maps are as accurate as possible, American map makers have devised "national map accuracy standards," which can be used as a test for any map made by any method. Since many modern maps are not made by classical surveying techniques, but rather by aerial images from airplane and satellite, and are plotted by machines instead of people, the standards are used to check their reliability. Maps that have passed the test can be labeled "This map complies with national map accuracy standards."

A new kind of map called the "orthophotographic map" is an aerial photograph that has been mechanically corrected to be true to scale (see Figure 24).

map symbols

All maps, large or small, copyrighted or not, and no matter what they show, must use some conventions in order to be intelligible. The two invariable conventions are orientation and scale; beyond that, there is a host of map symbols for use on different types of maps. Some of these are shown in Figure 27.

orientation and scale By convention, Earth maps are oriented with north toward the top of the map, although there are exceptions. A north arrow can be used to point in that direction; it should always appear on maps that do not have land grid derived from latitude and longitude (see Figures 25 and 26), and on maps that defy the north convention. On some large-scale maps, two arrows are shown (see Figure 27). One, usually pointing directly toward the top of the map, is "true north"; the other points toward "magnetic north." The "pole" around which our Earth spins is true north-south; the pull on

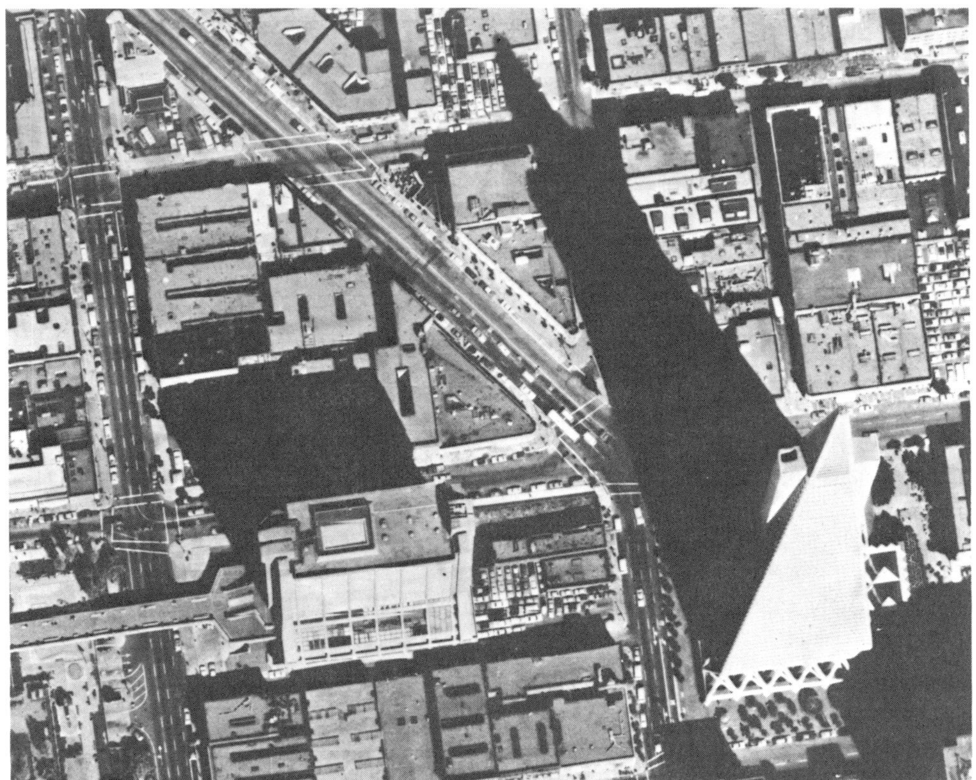

FIGURE 24 Here an orthophotographic map shows part of downtown San Francisco, on a scale of 1:1,200 (one inch equals 100 feet). The dramatic shadow of the Transamerica pyramid falls across Jackson Square historical district. The tip of the pyramid shadow points north; streets here do not run in cardinal directions.

This photomap has been corrected (hence the word "ortho" in its name). It can now be used for measurement, as camera distortion, aerial tilt, land elevation differences, and other alterations have been removed.

a compass is slightly off this center toward the magnetic north pole. For that reason, directions obtained by compass must be corrected to true north. The amount of correction, called "declination," varies from place to place on Earth, depending upon where each place is, relative to both the magnetic and true poles. The amount of declination in degrees should be shown.

Although it is possible to give an idea of scale by indicating known points or shapes (such as the shape of North America or Africa), most carefully drawn maps indicate scale by graphic or mathematical means, or both.

Scales expressed mathematically are ratios, or representative fractions. "1:24,000", for example, as seen on large-scale maps of the United States, means that 1 inch on the map is equal to 24,000 inches on the Earth, or 1 centimeter on the map is equal to 24,000 centimeters on the Earth. As 24,000 inches or centimeters are not amounts we are accustomed to dealing with, the scale is more understandable if translated into miles or kilometers. Read in feet, it would be 1 inch equals 2,000 feet; to obtain miles, reduce the fraction 1 inch equals 2,000/5,280 to 1 inch equals 0.3788 mile. In metric units, conversions are much simpler, as it is only necessary to divide by powers of ten: 1

Table 1. Commonly used map scales.

Scale	1 inch equals	1 cm equals
1:10,000	834 feet	100 meters
1:20,000	1,667 feet	200 meters
1:24,000	2,000 feet	240 meters
1:31,680	0.5 mile	317 meters
1:48,000	4,000 feet	480 meters
1:62,500	0.99 mile	625 meters
1:63,360	1 mile	634 meters
1:125,000	1.97 miles	1.25 kilometers
1:250,000	3.95 miles	2.5 kilometers
1:253,440	4 miles	2.53 kilometers
1:500,000	7.89 miles	5 kilometers
1:1,000,000	15.78 miles	10 kilometers
1:2,500,000	39.46 miles	25 kilometers
1:3,168,000	50 miles	31.68 kilometers
1:5,000,000	78.91 miles	50 kilometers
1:7,000,000	110.46 miles	70 kilometers
1:7,500,000	118.37 miles	75 kilometers
1:16,500,000	260.42 miles	165 kilometers

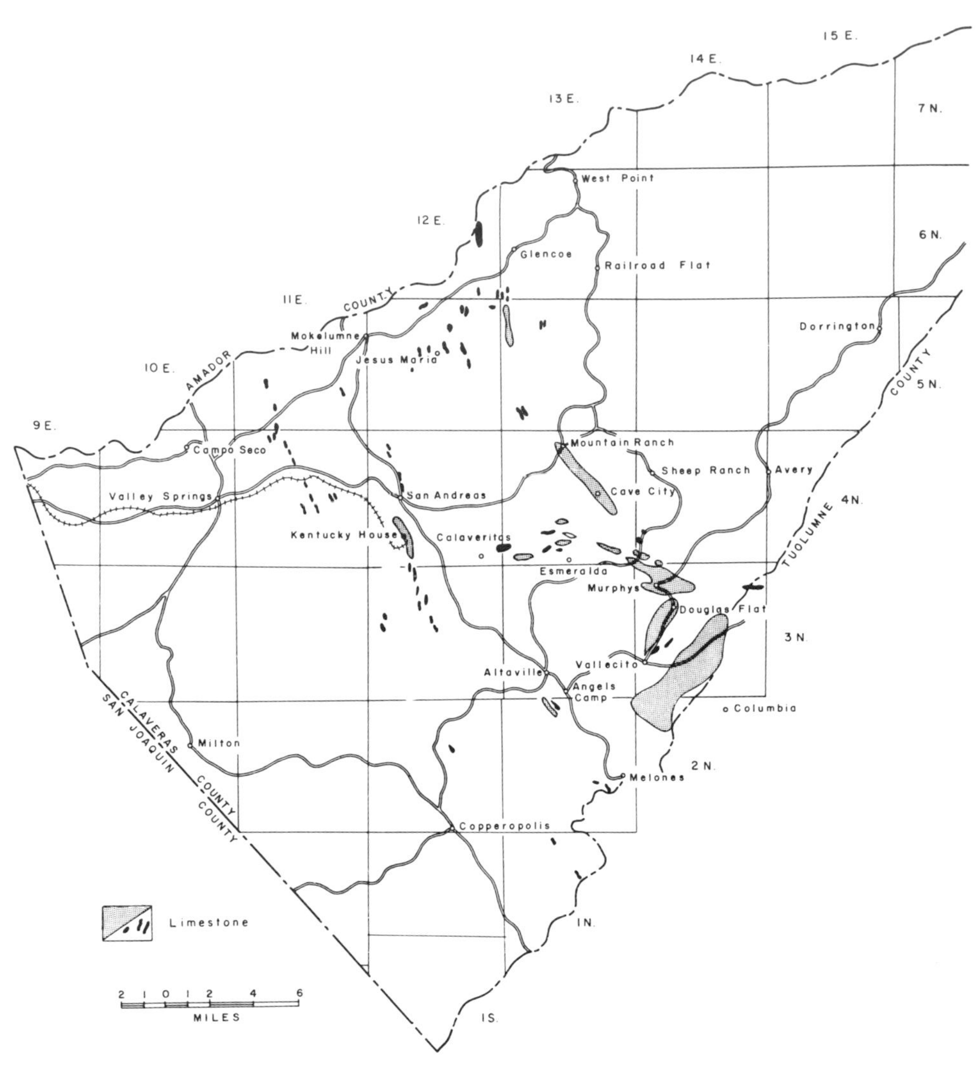

FIGURE 25 Map with a brief legend. Orientation is not specifically identified on this map, as the land net is shown. Several commonly used symbols appear on the map, but are not identified in the legend. These are interrupted lines marking political boundaries, double lines for roads, cross-hatched lines for railroads, and small circles for town sites. The caption to this map should specify its location, although a few literary readers will be able to locate "Calaveras County" and "Angels Camp" as the site of Mark Twain's jumping-frog story.

cm equals 24,000 cm; 1 cm equals 240 meters; 1 cm equals 0.24 kilometers.

Large-scale maps show much detail, as the ratio of the map to the land is much greater. Therefore, the larger the scale, the smaller the area shown on the same size of paper (large scale, large detail; small scale, small detail). A map of the city of San Francisco, for example, on the standard topographic quadrangle scale of 1:24,000 occupies a space 15 inches by 23 inches (38 cm by 58 cm). On a scale of

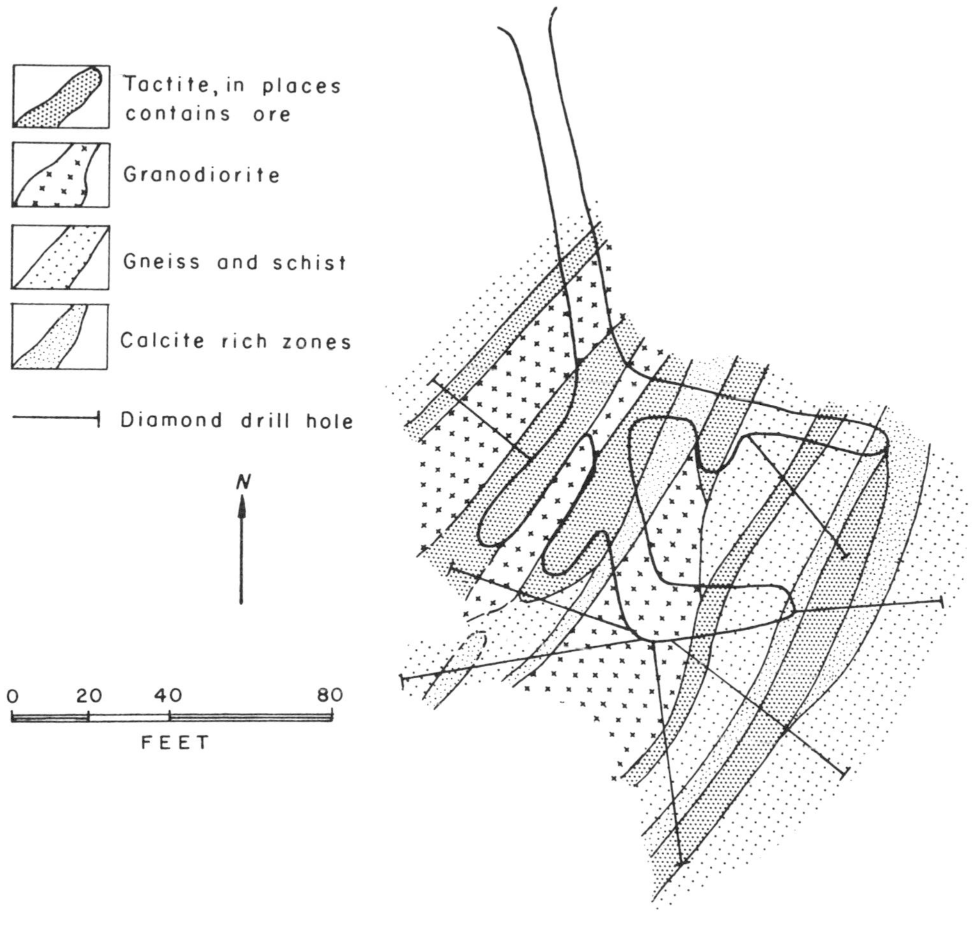

FIGURE 26

This map shows geology of part of a mine. Here, orientation and scale, as well as a legend, are given. Nevertheless, this is a diagram, not a map, as it gives no information that will enable the reader to go to the area to find any of the points shown. "It is not down in any map," said Ishmael, in *Moby Dick,* "true places never are." This is a true place, but not a true map.

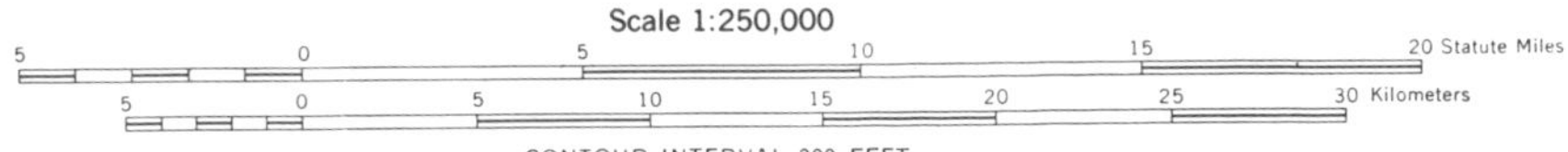

CONTOUR INTERVAL 200 FEET
WITH SUPPLEMENTARY CONTOURS AT 100 FOOT INTERVALS

GEOLOGIC MAP OF CALIFORNIA

OLAF P. JENKINS EDITION

LOS ANGELES SHEET

COMPILATION BY CHARLES W. JENNINGS AND RUDOLPH G. STRAND, 1969

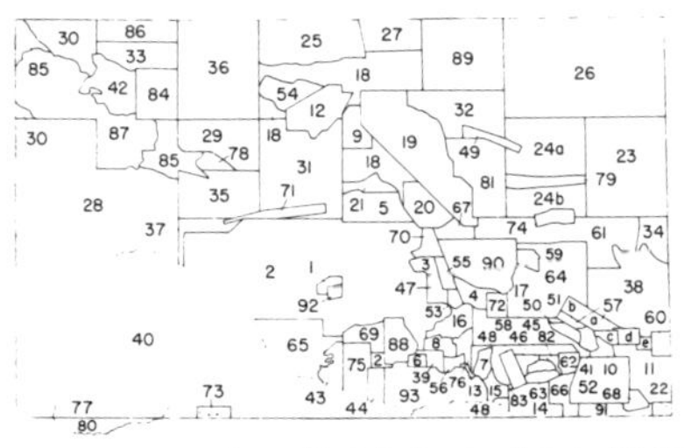

INDEX TO GEOLOGIC MAPPING

(COMPLETE INDEX ON EXPLANATORY DATA SHEET)

1. Baddley, E. R., 1954 2. Bailey, T. L., unpub. 3. Bain, R. J., unpub 4. Bishop, W. C., unpub. 5. Black, B. A., unpub. 6. Blackerby, B. A., unpub. 7. Brady, T. J., unpub. 8. Brown, G. E., unpub. 9. Burnett, J. L., unpub. 10. Byer, J. W., unpub. 11. California Dept. Water Resources, 1966. 12. Carman, M. F., Jr., 1964. 13. Carter, N. L., unpub. 14. Castle, R. O., 1960. 15. Champeny, J. D., unpub. 16. Conrad, S. D., unpub. 17. Corbato, C. E., 1963. 18-21. Crowell, J. C., and others. 22. Daviess, S. N., and Woodford, A. O., 1949. 23-37. Dibblee, T. W., Jr., and others. 38. Ehlig, P. L., unpub 39. Elam, J. G., unpub. 40. Emery, K. O., and Shepard, F. P., 1945*. 41. Frankian & Assoc., unpub. 42. Fritsche, A. E., unpub. 43. Gamble, J. H., unpub. 44. Guynes, G. E., unpub. 45. Hardey, G. W., unpub.; Elliott, J. L., unpub. 46. Harding, T. P., unpub. 47. Hetherington, G. E., unpub. 48. Hoots, H. W., 1931. 49. Jennings, C. W. and Dibblee, T. W., Jr., unpub. 50. Jennings, C. W. and Saul, R. B., unpub. 51. Johnston, R. L., unpub. 52. Lamar, D. L., unpub. 53. Levorsen, R. I., unpub. 54. Lofgren, G. E., unpub. 55. Martin, D. R., unpub. 56. McGill, J. T., unpub. 57-58. Metro. Water Dist. So. Calif., unpub. 59. Morrison, R. R., 1965. 60. Morton, D. M., unpub. 61. Muehlberger, W. R., 1958; Jahns, R. H. and Muehlberger, W. R., 1954. 62-63. Neuerburg, G. J. 64. Oakeshott, G. B., 1958. 65. Page, R. W., 1963. 66. Poland, J. F., Garrett, A. A. and Sinnott, A., 1959 67. Pollard, D. L., unpub. 68. Quarles, M., Jr., unpub. 69. Renke, D. F., unpub. 70. Robinson, B. B., unpub. 71. Rust, B. R., 1966. 72. Saul, R. B., unpub. 73. Scholl, D. W., 1960. 74. Silver, L. T., unpub. 75. Sonneman, H. W., unpub. 76. Soper, E. K., 1938. 77. Standard Oil Co. of Calif., unpub. 78. Stanford Geol. Survey, unpub. 79. Stanley, K. O., unpub. 80. Superior Oil Co., unpub.; Bremner, C. St. J., 1932; Rand, W. W., 1931. 81. Szatai, J. E., unpub.; Sams, R. H., unpub.; and Konigsberg, R. L., unpub. 82. Terpening, J. N., unpub. 83. Traxler, J. D., unpub. 84-87. Vedder, J. G., and others. 88. Weber, F. H., Jr., unpub. 89. Weise, J. H., 1950. 90. Winterer, E. L. and Durham, D. L., 1962. 91. Woodford, A. O., et al., 1954. 92. Yeats, R. S., 1965. 93. Yerkes, R. F., et al., unpub.

*40. Additional data on offshore breas, oil sand deposits, and offshore fault extensions from U.S. Geological Survey, Prof. Paper 679, Plates 1 and 2, (1969).

TOPOGRAPHIC BASE MAP

Prepared by the Army Map Service (KCLD), Corps of Engineers, U.S. Army, Washington, D.C. Compiled in 1959 from: United States Quadrangles, 1:24,000, 1:25,000, 1:50,000, U.S. Geological Survey and AMS, 1932-56. USC&GS Charts 5101, 1955; 5202, 1954. Planimetric detail revised by photo-planimetric methods. Control by USGS, USC&GS, USBR, U.S. Forest Service, Los Angeles City and County, U.S. Department of Agriculture, 29th Engineer Battalion, U.S. Army and Los Angeles Aqueduct Commission. Map field checked 1959.

Minor corrections and additions to culture by California Division of Mines and Geology. 1969

Land net prepared by U.S. Geological Survey

Submarine contours adapted from Shepard and Emery Special Paper No. 31, Geol. Soc. America

STATE OF CALIFORNIA
THE RESOURCES AGENCY
DEPARTMENT OF CONSERVATION

DIVISION OF MINES AND GEOLOGY

GEOLOGIC MAP OF CALIFORNIA
LOS ANGELES SHEET

FIGURE 27 Here is only part of the material appearing in the margin of one sheet of a complex special purpose map. The information, which was scattered outside the border, has been regrouped for this figure. All of it, which includes sources, scale, contour interval, and much more, was presented in addition to a very long legend printed in color. The entire map, which consists of 28 sheets, was lithographed in color, and when all sheets are assembled, it measures 14 feet by 7 feet (4.5 meters by 2 meters).

Although only four basic colors are used on a map such as this—yellow, red, blue, and black—by judicious mixing and the use of patterns, nearly 2,000 distinguishable colors can be printed. The effective use of more than a few colors requires specialized knowledge and experience. Compare this border information with that shown in Figure 25.

1:5,000,000 (a common world-atlas scale), the space required to letter the words "San Francisco" is larger than the space occupied by the city.

If you use a mathematical scale (1:24,000), be sure that the scale remains true during preparation and printing. Maps to be reproduced by means of photographic intermediate processes run the danger of having the scale altered. Check your map before and after it goes to press to be certain that the mathematical scale is still correct. In any case, you should also include a graphic scale, such as the one shown in Figure 27. It can be reduced or enlarged and still be true, provided that it is altered the same amount that the map is altered. All graphic scales should show metric units, or metric and American (English) units.

what to include

What you should put on your map depends upon its purpose. All maps must, of course, be generalized, as there is not room enough for everything actually on the ground ("the map is not the territory"). The smaller the scale, the greater the amount of generalization. Decide what you wish to show, and show that as clearly and sparsely as possible. The borders of a map, or unused areas in it, should carry legend, sources, and the names of those who helped prepare it. For simple index maps, this may be only one line; for more complex, special-purpose maps, a great deal of information may be required (see Figure 27).

remember your user

Beware of provincialism in preparing copy for the map, legend, and caption. True, each map is of a local area, but if your readers knew as much about that area as you do, you might not need to make a map. The European habit of naming unfamiliar places by names similar to those of the homeland has caused confusion; that, coupled with the human habit of identifying "White Mountains," "Table Mountains," and "Snowy Mountains" in a variety of languages, makes geographic identity difficult unless your readers know exactly what part of the Earth your map presents. Does an African or American reader know clearly the difference between Inner Hebrides, Outer Hebrides, and New Hebrides? Between South Wales and New South Wales? Can Europeans correctly identify Mexico and New Mexico, California and Baja California?

Avoid abbreviations. The U.S. Postal Service may recognize the geographic separation of AL, AK, AZ, AR, and Alta, but does a foreign reader know even which country is meant? Although the caption or title to each map may not require it, be sure that somewhere in your text you identify not only the county, province, or state, but the country, and, if necessary, continent that you are discussing.

cartography and printing

Once you have organized the information for your map, select a qualified cartographer to make the final printer's copy. Maps to be printed in color require special overlays (at least one for each color) and perfect registration. You must decide what to show and what to emphasize, but let your cartographer organize, plan, and arrange the map. Be available for consultation, and be sure to inform her or him by what method and in what colors the map is to be printed. You may need to make a colored mock-up of the finished map, but remember that what the cartographer prepares for the printer will be entirely black, or red and black, both of which are black to the camera. Your final printed map will, of course, be in color.

The finished product, ready for press, may consist of two or more parts (base and overlays), each to be printed in a separate color. To print a map with black lettering and orange roads, for example, the cartographer prepares two sheets: one with lettering in black ink to be printed in black, the other with black lines representing roads to be printed in orange. From these, two separate printing plates will be made, one for orange, one for black. Each piece of paper is run through the press once for an orange imprint, once for black. In large presses that can print more than one color, the colors may be printed in quick succession, but one plate is required for each ink. Both the orange lines and black letters must be printed precisely in the right place (be in "perfect registration") if the map is to be correct and legible.

Your cartographer can letter directly on your map by hand or machine, or she can paste on words and letters from prepared copy. Art stores stock alphabets for use in letter-by-letter spelling; whole words, sentences, or blocks of copy can be purchased from typesetters or set on photocomposition machines. Machine lettering, like art-store letters and printed copy, is reliable and predictable, but cannot compare with artistic hand lettering.

As the map will probably be prepared considerably larger than it will be printed, the lettering must be appropriately larger. Figure 3 (page 26) shows lettering reduced by different amounts. Note that letters and lines should be thick enough to avoid fading, but thin and open enough that they will not blur or close up in printing.

checking and rechecking

When the cartographer has completed the maps, you must check them for completeness and correctness.

Simple maps should contain
- Orientation (north)
- Scale
- Source (if needed)
- Caption or legend, or both.

More complex maps may also need
- Contour interval and datum
- Projection used
- Author's or compiler's name, contributors
- Sponsors, draftsmen, cartographers, so labeled (unless credits are handled in another manner)
- Name of publisher and place of publication
- Series, or sheet identification, or both.

The legend should show
- Explanation of all patterns
- Explanation of symbols.

All maps should be checked to make certain that spelling and numbers are correct, and that overlays, if any, are in proper registration. Doublecheck now to certify the scale and orientation.

When the maps have been completed to your satisfaction, you will be required to read them again at the proofing stage (see pages 132-138) to recheck the scale, registration, orientation, and reduction.

digging deeper

Base maps for the world and its parts are available from a variety of sources. Some are commercial or private (including scientific societies), many are public. *International Maps and Atlases in Print,* edited by Kenneth L. Winch (1974; Bowker, New York), lists sources of maps by country, including both governmental agency and private enterprise.

An uncopyrighted atlas of most of the world can be assembled by obtaining *World Aeronautical Charts,* on a scale of 1:1,000,000. These are published by the U.S. Department of Commerce, Riverdale, Maryland 20840. Each section is sold separately. *A Catalog of Aeronautical Charts and Related Publications* is available on request from the U.S. Department of Commerce; it lists, in addition to World Aeronautical Charts, Global Navigation Charts, Operational Navigational Charts, Jet Navigational Charts, Universal Water Charts, and many others.

The Department of Commerce periodically issues a *Nautical Chart Catalog,* which lists charts of the coastal areas of the United States and its Territories, as well as other maps available from the Department. Among other maps are outline maps on various projections and scales, U.S. base maps, and bathymetric maps.

Special-topic world atlases have been planned and in part published under the sponsorship of the United Nations Educational, Scientific, and Cultural Organization. Among them are geologic, geographic, ecological, and climate maps of all continents on a variety of scales. A catalog of this worldwide effort may be obtained from Unesco Publications Center, Division of Unipub Inc., P.O. Box 433, New York, N.Y. 10016.

For the Western Hemisphere, the basic maps issued for land areas are topographic. An index of Canadian topographic maps may be obtained from the Surveys and Mapping Branch, Department of Energy, Mines and Resources, Ottawa, Ontario, Canada. Sources of Mexican, Central American, and South American topographic maps are listed in *International Maps and Atlases.*

Basic mapping of the United States is principally the responsibility of the United States Geological Survey. However, many government agencies publish maps. A list of who publishes what is available from the U.S. Geological Survey. Ask for the pamphlet, *Types of Maps Published by Government Agencies.*

The *National Atlas of the United States,* issued by the U.S. Geological Survey in 1970, is a 765-page work, combining maps showing general characteristics (relief, climate, geology, etc.) and special topics. It, as well as other maps published by the U.S. Geological Survey, is listed in its catalog, *Publications of the Geological Survey,* available on request from the U.S. Geological Survey, Stop 329, Reston, Virginia 22092. Among the maps issued are outline maps, physical divisions, river surveys, land classifications, oil and gas investigations, and geophysical maps and charts.

For each of the 50 states, as well as Puerto Rico, Guam, American Samoa, and the Virgin Islands, a special index of topographic maps is published at intervals by the U.S. Geological Survey. These list all topographic quadrangle maps in print, special maps and sheets, maps of national parks and monuments, and base maps of the United States. The lists may be obtained from the Branch of Distribution, U.S. Geological Survey, 1200 South Eads Street, Arlington, Virginia 22202 for areas east of the Mississippi River, and Minnesota, Puerto Rico, and the Virgin

Islands. For western areas, including Alaska, Hawaii, Louisiana, Guam, and American Samoa, write to U.S. Geological Survey, Branch of Distribution, Denver Federal Center, Denver, Colorado 80225.

Other U.S. government agencies, also, publish maps for various purposes. The U.S. Forest Service publishes planimetric maps of the forest areas; the U.S. Bureau of Land Management publishes maps of recreation areas under its jurisdiction. The U.S. Army, which once had responsibility for all national mapping, still publishes many maps, some of which are available to the public. Other mapping agencies include the Department of Housing & Urban Development and the Central Intelligence Agency.

Many books have been published on the history of maps, map projections, cartography, and various phases of geography. Books on drafting and technical illustration also give a little information on map making. Special instructions for such government agencies as the U.S. Geological Survey have been issued for their own internal use; they are of great value to the practicing cartographer—provided he can obtain them—but the general scientist will have little need of them.

One book on preparing maps for publication is outstanding; it covers modern methods from planning, layout, design, and drafting through various printing processes: *Cartographic Design and Production,* by J.S. Keates (1973; Halsted Press, John Wiley and Sons, Inc., New York). It is useful to the author, who needs to recognize the complexities of map production, as well as to the working cartographer.

A reference and reading book on map making with a warm and informal approach is David Greenhood's *Mapping* (1964; University of Chicago Press). It has an appendix filled with useful tables: scale conversions, distances, dimensions, and much more.

Geography and Cartography; a Reference Handbook by C.B. Muriel Lock (1976; Linnet Books, Hamden, Connecticut) is a very useful bibliographic tool. It contains annotated references and information and has a thorough index.

key points

In making maps

- Select a suitable base
- Determine orientation and scale
- Identify sources, authors, etc.
- Use legend to clarify map symbols and patterns

14
LISTING: making tables

Almost all papers and books of a technical or scientific nature contain tables, as that is a very efficient way of presenting information. All of us have had wide experience in reading tables—bus schedules, recipes, telephone directories—but few have had wide experience in constructing them. It is a skill that requires thought and care. "What shall I present?" is the first question you should ask, followed by "How shall I present it?"

table versus narrative

Make a table when it will make your data easier to read, or will bring out relationships not easily discernible in words. For example, of these two presentations, the table is clearer and more usable:

> County tax levy on property was 1, rate 2.32 amount $255.20; regulation of open space levy 1, rate .100, amount $11.00; flood-control, levy 1, rate .232, amount $25.52; mosquito-abatement levy 1, rate .020, amount $2.20; pollution-control levy 1, rate .015, amount $1.65; transit-district levy 1, rate .050, amount $5.50; hospital levy 1, rate .092, amount $10.12; elementary-school levy 1, rate 2.794, amount $307.34; high-school levy 1, rate 1.885, amount $207.35; community-college levy 1, rate 1.053, amount $115.83; school special-education fund levy 1, rate .289, amount $31.79; city tax levy 1, rate 2.650, amount $291.50; special-assessments levy 3, amount $40.80; total tax rate 11.500; total tax, $1,305.80.

RATES AND DISTRIBUTION OF AMOUNTS BY TAXING AGENCIES			
TAXING AGENCY	LEVY	RATE	AMOUNT
COUNTY	1	2.320	$255.20
REG. OPEN SPACE	1	.100	11.00
FLOOD CONTROL	1	.232	25.52
MOSQUITO ABATE	1	.020	2.20
POLLUTION CONTROL	1	.015	1.65
TRANSIT DISTRICT	1	.050	5.50
HOSPITAL	1	.092	10.12
ELEMENTARY SCHOOL	1	2.794	307.34
HIGH SCHOOL	1	1.885	207.35
COMMUNITY COLLEGE	1	1.053	115.83
SCHOOLS SPECIAL ED.	1	.289	31.79
CITY	1	2.650	291.50
SPECIAL ASSESSMENTS	3		40.80
TOTAL		11.500	1,305.80

However, tables are expensive to set in type, and your publisher may balk at a large number of them. If you have a great many tables, or tables that are very detailed, or if your tables are of a size larger than will fit on a double-page spread, you may file them in a data retrieval center (such as the National Technical Information Service) rather than include them in your publication.

Use tables to supplement, not duplicate, your text. Discuss only the highlights; allow your readers to ferret out details for themselves. Bear in mind that your tables, because of their size and shape, may not be placed exactly where you would like them. Your publisher will try to fit them in where they should go, but this is not always possible. Therefore, make each table independent—understandable whether or not the text is nearby.

You may, of course, refer to the table in the text, but use its number if possible (e.g., "see Table 2"); do not say "the following table" or "the table above"—after all, it may not be following, or above, when the book is printed.

orientation

Once you have decided what to present in tables, try to organize the information in its most logical form. If you can, arrange tables so that they can be read in the same direction as the text. Tables turned broadside (at right angles to the text) can be used, but in this position they are awkward and disruptive for the reader. Furthermore, unless they occupy the entire page, some space will be wasted.

After you have constructed a preliminary version of a table, study it to see if you have presented it in the best way. Sometimes you can improve upon your tabular logic by switching the material presented horizontally with that presented vertically. Try to group units in the column heads or along the stub for clarity (see Figure 28).

If words or numbers in a table will not fit in the space when printed horizontally and cannot be abbreviated sufficiently, they are often turned vertically. In such cases it is conventional to orient them as if rotated counterclockwise; thus in order to read the entire table the reader need turn the page clockwise only slightly. For the same reason, if an entire table will not fit horizontally, it, too, will be rotated counterclockwise.

However, if a line within a table is rotated counterclockwise and the table, too, is rotated in the same direction, some lines will read upside down. That inconveniences the reader, who must turn the entire page clockwise more than 90 degrees in order to read those lines with

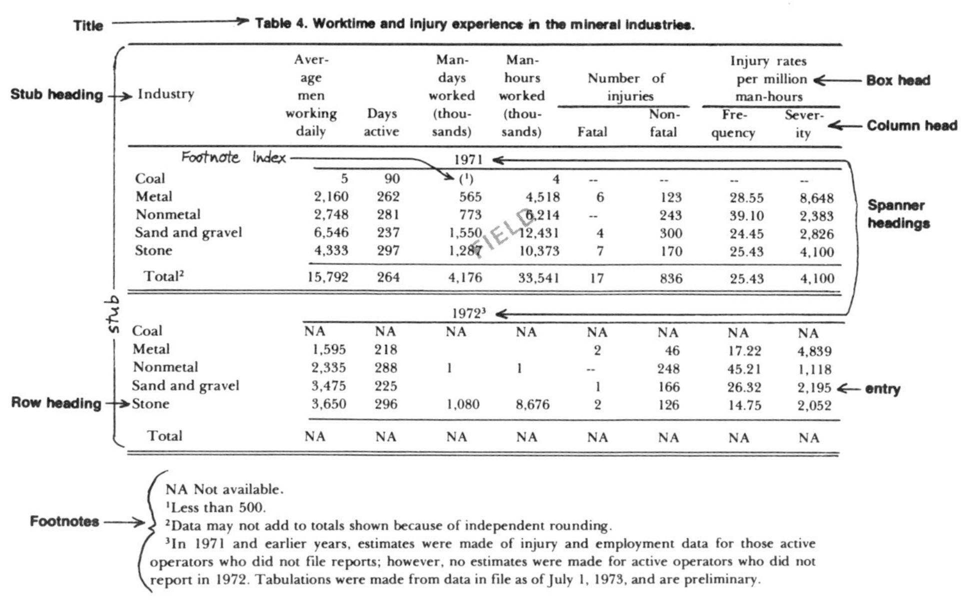

Table 4. Worktime and injury experience in the mineral industries.

Industry	Average men working daily	Days active	Man-days worked (thousands)	Man-hours worked (thousands)	Number of injuries		Injury rates per million man-hours	
					Fatal	Nonfatal	Frequency	Severity
			1971					
Coal	5	90	(1)	4	--	--	--	--
Metal	2,160	262	565	4,518	6	123	28.55	8,648
Nonmetal	2,748	281	773	6,214	--	243	39.10	2,383
Sand and gravel	6,546	237	1,550	12,431	4	300	24.45	2,826
Stone	4,333	297	1,287	10,373	7	170	25.43	4,100
Total[2]	15,792	264	4,176	33,541	17	836	25.43	4,100
			1972[3]					
Coal	NA	NA	NA	NA	NA	NA	NA	NA
Metal	1,595	218			2	46	17.22	4,839
Nonmetal	2,335	288	1	1	--	248	45.21	1,118
Sand and gravel	3,475	225			1	166	26.32	2,195
Stone	3,650	296	1,080	8,676	2	126	14.75	2,052
Total	NA	NA	NA	NA	NA	NA	NA	NA

NA Not available.
[1]Less than 500.
[2]Data may not add to totals shown because of independent rounding.
[3]In 1971 and earlier years, estimates were made of injury and employment data for those active operators who did not file reports; however, no estimates were made for active operators who did not report in 1972. Tabulations were made from data in file as of July 1, 1973, and are preliminary.

FIGURE 28 Parts of a table.

any ease. In such cases you or your editor should break with convention and turn the offending lines clockwise.

Be sure to identify all units of measurement (troy ounces, long tons, liters, hectares) in the most convenient place. For example, the unit of measurement in this heading

Production
(in kilograms)

1974 1975 1976

is easier to find than if "in kilograms" were given in a footnote, particularly if the table is long.

parallelism

Use parallelism in constructing your tables—in designations, as well as in units of measurement. Here is an example of poor parallelism, pointed out by the *Publication Manual of the American Psychological Association*:

Trait
Intelligent
Talks a lot
Aggression

The editors of that manual suggest that rewording would improve the listing:

Trait
Intelligent
Talkative
Aggressive

rules

Vertical and horizontal lines—called rules—that separate entries are used to make reading easier. As vertical rules are often costly (depending upon how the type is set), publishers do not like to include them unless they are absolutely necessary. Unless you are preparing a thesis or a paper that will not be set in type (that is, if your typing is to be photographed as is), do not rule tables vertically or draw many horizontal lines; leave that to your publisher.

In tables using statement forms, avoid periods if possible. If you cannot, try to use periods uniformly throughout the table. Also, be sure to use the same abbreviations consistently, if at all, and be certain that your readers will know what the abbreviations mean.

titles

Table titles should be as short as possible, but explanatory. Include the table number as the first item. Do not repeat material in the spanner headings, box headings, column headings, or stub headings. For example, in Figure 28, had the title been "Mean of man days and hours worked, number and rates of fatal and nonfatal injuries for coal, metal, and nonmetal mines and sand and gravel and stone quarries for 1971 and 1972," it would have repeated information in the table. On the other hand, a more telegraphic title, such as "Injuries," leaves out vital information.

If you have trouble constructing a comprehensive table title, ask yourself: "Am I presenting only one idea in this table?" If you find you have several ideas combined, consider dividing them into two or more tables. A table should be like a paragraph: it should have one topic.

Some publishers require table titles to be typed above the table; others below. If you do not know which style to use, type the title at the top of the table, where it will be printed.

typing tables

Do not underline any headings or other parts of the table unless you have generic or specific names or other material that requires italics. Even so, if your table is principally a list of genera and species, it is sometimes permissible to omit italics: however, to avoid confusion, underline all names of genera and species, but no other words. Your designer will decide the style of type to use.

In typing tables, be careful of alignment. Numbers should fall under one another vertically in each group, with the decimal point in the same position:

86.5
13.71
0.1

Use commas in all numbers of 1,000 or more:

25,684
2,108
764

If your figures include ranges, align the first decimal point in each entry, if possible:

97.5
80.3-81
85.1-86.7
80-92

In this example, if equally significant figures had been determined for all entries, the table might have read:

97.5	or	98
80.3-81.0		80-81
85.1-86.7		85-87
80.0-92.0		80-92

If you did not determine the figures yourself, you cannot exceed the accuracy of your source.

In tables with standard deviations, align the standard deviation first, then the decimal points left and right:

20.3	σ	2.5
713	σ	50
7.6	σ	0.21

Some publishers do not use a zero ahead of the decimal point; others prefer it.

abbreviations

Long, rounded numbers may be abbreviated by so indicating in the column heads. For example:

Commodity	**Value**
Coal	$25,000,000
Oil	2,647,000,000
Natural gas	1,312,000,000

can be written as:

Commodity	**Value** (in millions of dollars)
Coal	25
Oil	2,647
Natural gas	1,312

or:

Commodity	**Value** (in millions)
Coal	$ 25
Oil	2,647
Natural gas	1,312

You can also abbreviate units other than dollars that are inconveniently large or small if you use proper column heads. For example, "in thousands of metric tons" will eliminate three zeros in the entire column; "ppm" (parts per million) will eliminate six. However, in using such headings as "$x10^{-3}$" or "10^{4}", be aware that two conventions exist. One indicates that the number has been multiplied by the factor given, the other that it should be. Do not use this method unless you make it quite clear which you mean. The Council of Biology Editors recommends that the multiplying factor be associated with the number, rather than with the unit of measure, to avoid this confusion. A sample column head might then read "102g," and under it, the figure 1.2 (indicating 120 grams). An alternative is to write out the heading:

Weight
(in hundreds of grams)
1.2

In presenting dollar figures, percentage, or other lists of numbers that are added or subtracted, double check all arithmetic. Nothing will detract from an otherwise good presentation more quickly than an inaccurately figured sum, no matter how trivial that sum may be.

citing sources

Footnotes are an integral part of almost every table. Use them to give information on the table as a whole, to give information on specific items, and to cite sources. One way to cite sources for tables:

For sources quoted directly: "From John Doe, 'Life in the West,' *Ecotimes,* vol. 1, no. 1, p. 1, 341. Copyright, 1975, by *Ecotimes.* Printed by permission. For tables that are modified: "After J. Doe, "Life in the West," *Ecotimes,* vol. 1, no. 1, p. 1,341."

A table, copied in its entirety, is essentially an extended quotation; for that reason, you should obtain a letter of permission from the copyright holder. A letter of request similar to that used for figures (see page 45) will serve for tables as well. Be sure to cite both the author and the copyright holder in the credit footnote.

If only part of your table is from another source, or if you have constructed a table using several sources, cite each source by such a footnote statement as, "The figures in column 1 are from ———." If you do not know whether or not you need to write a letter asking permission from a publisher to quote the figures, err on the side of courtesy and safety: write one.

digging deeper

Study and practice are the keys to learning to make good tables. However, the way in which tables are printed varies from publisher to publisher. To learn how a particular publishing house handles tables, you should consult its publications and its stylebook, if there is one. Most scientific societies have stylebooks of their own or use a published one.

If comprehensiveness is what you want in a stylebook, try the *Style Manual of the U.S. Government Printing Office* (January 1973; Washington D.C.) or *A Manual of Style* (12th edition, 1969; University of Chicago Press). If your field is education, consider the *NEA Style Manual for Writers and Editors* (National Education Association, 1966; Washington, D.C.), If the biological sciences, the *CBE Style Manual* by the Council of Biology Editors (3d edition, 1972; American Institute of Biological Sciences, Washington, D.C.); if chemistry, the *Handook for Authors of Papers in the Research Journals of the American Chemical Society* (1965; Washington, D.C.); if physics, the *Style Manual for Guidance in Preparation of Papers for Journals Published by the American Institute of Physics* (1962; New York), if psychology, the *Publication Manual of the American Psychological Association* (2nd edition, 1974; Washington, D.C.), if mathematics, *Manual for Authors of Mathematical Papers* (1962; American Mathematical Society, Providence, Rhode Island); if geology, *Geowriting,* edited by Wendell Cochran, Peter Fenner, and Mary Hill (2d edition, 1974; American Geological Institute; Falls Church, Virginia); if geophysics, *JGR Style* (1968; American Geophysical Union; Washington, D.C.). Widely used in academic publishing is the *MLA Style Sheet* (2nd edition, 1970; Modern Language Association of America; New York). A sound style book for general usage is the *New York Times Manual of Style and Usage,* subtitled *A Desk Book of Guidelines for Writers and Editors* and edited by Lewis Jordan (1976; Quadrangle/The New York Times Book Company).

key points

Use tables to
- condense
- clarify
- supplement

Construct good tables by
- selecting one topic per table
- using the most logical form
- being consistent in details
- citing sources

15
FINISHING: adding front and back matter

Henry Thoreau once wrote that when chopping a pile of kindling you can chop the big sticks first, or you can chop the little sticks first, but sooner or later you must chop them all. As an author you may never have to chop all the sticks described in this section, but you should know about them and be ready to chop when asked.

front matter

Very few books have all the elements of "front matter"—the material appearing between the cover and the beginning of the main text—but when one does the sequence may run like this: half-title page, publisher's card, title page, copyright, colophon, dedication, acknowledgments, foreword (or preface, or both), table of contents, list of illustrations, introduction, second half-title page.

Your book may need all those elements or only a few. As to the order, there is nothing sacrosanct and little that is required, although copyright regulations are fairly strict. Your publisher's designer and editor will try to reconcile custom, economy, appearance, and convenience to your readers.

half-title page

The half-title page (also called "bastard title page") is an endangered species, but as it is not particularly functional it may not deserve protection. At best it only repeats a part of the title appearing on the real title page.

The publisher's card (sometimes "ad card") might better be called the author's card, for it is usually headed something like this: "Other books by the same author." Sometimes the heading is more restrictive, as in "Other books by the same author available from this publisher." In any case, the content and purpose are apparent. Usually the publisher's card is on a left-hand page far forward, perhaps facing the title page.

publisher's card

The title page must carry the full title of the book, including subtitle, and almost always includes the author's name. Beyond that, there may be various credits (such as the name of a translator or photographer), the imprint (publisher, city, year), the publisher's trademark, a quotation, an illustration . . .

title page

Copyright regulations require that the copyright notice appear on the title page or on the first page after that. The second option is commonly taken, so much so that this page may be called the copyright page. The notice should take the form "Copyright © 1978 William Kaufmann, Inc." The notice is mandatory for any publication dated earlier than Jan. 1, 1978, the effective date of the new U.S. copyright law. After that date the notice is not absolutely required but is still very important: do not fail to include it.

copyright notice

Under the old copyright law, you or your publisher would, after publication, file claim for copyright, using forms obtained from the Register of Copyrights (Library of Congress, Washington, D.C., 20559). Such copyrights are good for 28 years, and may be extended.

Under the new copyright law, copyright takes effect with the act of creation, giving you statutory protection from the beginning (under the old law you would rely on common law, and sometimes on state laws, for protection of your manuscript until it was actually published). However, for full protection you must register your copyright with the Register of Copyrights. Such a copyright in your own name will be good for your lifetime plus 50 years.

the new law

If you write a book (or other work) as a part of your job (as a "work for hire"), the copyright will be in your employer's name and will be good for 75 years. However, there is no provision for government-held copyright.

In recent years the copyright page has become a catchall for technical information such as the Library of Congress Cataloging in Publication Data (known as C.I.P.; this is, in effect, a copy of the catalog card that will

C.I.P. ISBN and ISSN

represent your book in the Library of Congress); the International Standard Book Number (or ISBN, which is a unique number for each edition of each book); the International Standard Serial Number (the ISSN, which most often applies to serial journals but also applies to books in a series, so that your book may bear both an ISBN and an ISSN); and the colophon. Your publisher must obtain the C.I.P., the ISBN, and the ISSN. Even the dedication and acknowledgments may be found on the copyright page.

colophon

Historically, the colophon began as a device identifying the printer, and in this function it still appears on the title page as the publisher's trademark. Later the colophon moved to the extreme back of the book, where it may take the form of a brief statement about the design of the book, including such things as the name and characteristics of the main typeface (and sometimes others) and the name of its editor and designer, the names of the paper, typesetter and typesetting process, printer, binder and production manager. Now it sometimes appears on the copyright page.

dedication

The dedication is a sort of private message, publicly displayed, from the author to another person or persons. It is so personal that it takes a wide variety of forms; see the four-page dedication of *Bertie Wooster Sees it Through,* by P.G. Wodehouse, which amounts to a spoof on dedications. Almost anything goes.

acknowledgments

Acknowledgments (of help in preparing the book) may appear separately, or as a part of the foreword, or even at the end of the book.

foreword (preface)

The foreword consists of a discussion by the author of how and why the book was written; alternatively, it may consist of similar comments by another person.

table of contents

The table of contents is a functional device too often neglected by author and designer, who thereby fail the reader. It usually begins as the author's preliminary outline. This may explain why Roman numerals sometimes precede chapter titles, but if that is their origin and sole purpose they should be abandoned as a needless distraction. It may be no more than a list of chapter titles, commonly with page numbers, but it can and should be much more informative.

The contents page may also list subsections within chapters, each with its own page number. It can give a précis of each chapter, using full sentences, or it can give a running list of topics covered (an old-fashioned but still useful device).

Note that the table of contents is related to the index. The former is a device for proceeding from the general to the particular, and the latter is a device for proceeding from the particular to the general. You should make up each with the other in mind.

list of illustrations

The list of illustrations seems to be falling into disuse, perhaps because it so often does little for the reader but serves mainly as a checklist for the author and editor. You should include such a list in your finished book only if it will help your readers.

introduction

The introduction should concern your book itself, telling for whom it is intended (this important information is too often omitted) and how the reader may use it.

The second half-title page may help the designer avoid starting the text on a left-hand page, or it may indicate that the front matter is so extensive that someone feared that the reader would forget the book's title. In any case it separates the end of the front matter and the beginning of the text.

back matter

Now for the back matter, which follows the text and usually appears in this order: appendix (or appendixes), reference notes, bibliography (or list of references, or both), glossary, and index. (But see "colophon" above.)

appendix

Whether you need an appendix may be hard to decide. For example, a chapter may call for a long table; if that table constitutes a major interruption of the text, perhaps you should make an appendix of it. However, you should not needlessly force the reader to flip repeatedly to and from the chapter involved. When it is difficult to decide whether to use an a appendix or not, your solution may be to rewrite the chapter in order to reduce the number of times the reader must turn to the appendix. Or you might put the table at the end of the chapter. In any case you must make clear to the reader how text and table relate to each other.

reference notes

Reference notes usually consist of explanatory material too technical or too extensive for use as footnotes. They pose a major problem in devising convenient cross-references with the text.

bibliography

You may want to distinguish between "list of references" and "bibliography", the former consisting of only the publications you have actually cited in your text, and the latter consisting of those you deem useful to your readers. However, you may want to list instead the publications you used in the course of your research and writing, or you may want to make up a list that combines those categories in some way. Perhaps your best course is to specify, briefly, what your list consists of.

You may have a bibliography (or whatever) at the end of each chapter, or one at the end of the book. If at the end of the book it may be in one unit, or it may be arranged by chapters, or it may be arranged by subtopics.

In any case consistency is essential. There are many standards for bibliographic citations, but here are the elements in one order: author's name (family name and given name) or the editor's name; publication date; title; kind of publication (if special, such as abstract, editorial, or photo); series title (such as journal or symposium issue); volume number (and part and issue number if pertinent); publisher's name and address; pagination. Unless there is a specific reason, as when your journal editor requires a certain style on submission, spell out everything; abbreviations save some space but they sacrifice much time spent in checking and translating. It is easier for the editor to abbreviate according to his style than to decipher your system and *then* abbreviate.

glossary

If your text includes many terms that will be new to your readers, a glossary may save time for them even if you define "new" terms as you go along. The number of such terms may determine how you should treat them (a separate glossary at the end of each chapter may be desirable). Consider defining each term where it occurs in the index.

index

As to the index: you are the expert on your own book, and so you are the prime candidate for indexing it. However, indexing is a difficult job, and there are many ways of doing it. Also, you cannot finish indexing until shortly before printing because it is only at the page-proof stage that you have the book's page numbers. But you can read up on the subject (start with pages 139-148) and consider the various kinds of indexes and how yours is likely to be used. Again, ponder whether you should define new terms where they fall in the index itself, and keep the contents page in mind.

Finally: if a few blank pages fall at the end of the book, leave them blank, or they may be distributed elsewhere in the book, such as between appendixes. At any rate, do not call attention to them by asking the printer to set "notes" at the top.

writing an abstract

If you're writing a technical report: nearly every technical report must have an abstract—"a condensation and concentration of the *essential information* in the paper."

Many people believe that the abstract is the most important part of a technical paper, and most agree that at least fifty times as many people read the abstract as read the paper itself. To write a good abstract, use the active voice, tell what you have discovered and not what your paper is about, condense and concentrate "the essential information."

digging deeper

Bookmaking: the Illustrated Guide to Design and Production, by Marshall Lee (1965; R.R. Bowker Co.; New York), discusses point by point the various elements that may make up a book. *Bookmaking* itself is a good example of innovative but sound design.

There is no generally accepted standard for style of bibliographic citations—that is, the order and abbreviation of their elements. However, a committee of the American National Standards Institute is working on guidelines, and some individual publications have their own standards (see page 96-97). Perhaps the most widely used standard in the sciences is that of Chemical Abstracts Service, Columbus, Ohio; you may be able to use it directly or adapt it to your needs.

"A Scrutiny of the Abstract, II," by Kenneth K. Landes, is reprinted in *Geowriting: a Guide to Writing, Editing, and Printing in Earth Science,* edited by Wendell Cochran, Peter Fenner, and Mary Hill (2nd edition, 1974; American Geological Institute; Falls Church, Virginia). Landes's "Scrutiny" is essential reading for anyone about to write an abstract.

key points

You may have to deal with each of these front matter and back matter elements:

- half-title page
- title page
- copyright notice
- C.I.P.
- ISBN
- ISSN
- colophon
- dedication

- acknowledgments
- foreword (or preface)
- table of contents
- list of illustrations
- introduction
- abstract
- appendixes
- reference notes
- bibliography
- glossary
- index

16 MARKETING: finding a publisher

Whether your literary creation is still merely an idea, or whether it has flowered into a thick manuscript, replete with illustrations, you will need to market it. If you have written a highly technical treatise, you should select a journal that specializes in your field; if you have written a "popular" work aimed at every reader over six, you will still be obliged to find a willing publisher.

finding a publisher

Let's consider books. Some books are written on assignment for an employer. *Salt in California,* a technical work on the harvesting of table salt from ponds evaporated by the heat of the Sun, was such a book, assigned by a state geological survey to a member of its own staff. The author was told what to write about, and when the manuscript was due. When it was nearly completed, his employer decided on the best format, selecting one of several used by the agency.

Or, a publisher may ask you to write a book on a subject in which you are expert. Very often, in such cases, the publisher will specify the length and format, perhaps to match others in a series.

outlines and sample chapter

One way for you to find a publisher is to send an outline to a prospective one, perhaps with a sample chapter from the book. If he (or she) likes your idea and your writing, he or a member of his staff will probably want to discuss it with you, and, if all goes well, will end up by offering you a contract—something we will have more to say about later.

complete manuscripts

Another way to find a publisher is to wait until your book is essentially complete. Then you can send it "cold" to a publisher. If you have to do this very many times, your manuscript may become tattered or even lost; so a letter inquiring as to a publisher's interest may save you time, money, and headaches.

Perhaps you will be unsuccessful in locating a publisher because your manuscript is "too technical," "too local," or has "too limited an audience." Publishers have all sorts of answers—some patently excuses, some legitimate reasons—for rejecting manuscripts. Most publishers and editors, believe it or not, do not like to be unkind (for one thing, it loses readers and sales), so they will rarely say, "It's a bad book," although they may well think just that.

Of the 40,000 different books published in 1975, about 90 percent were nonfiction—as this book is. The market for nonfiction is good; if your book is also good, you have an excellent chance of finding a willing publisher.

specialty publishers

Remember that publishers and publisher's editors tend to specialize. Williams and Wilkins, for example, publishes professional books in medicine, life sciences, and mathematics; the University of Oklahoma Press is known for its Western Americana; W.H. Freeman is best known for earth-science texts. Therefore, it may be best to search for a publisher who knows your field, but bear in mind that he may already be committed to a rival book. On the other hand, a publisher who has no offerings on your subject may wish to expand.

If you do not know any publishers, ask friends who have published to tell about their experience. They can give you names and addresses, as well as tell you stories of their publishing experiences. Also, you can find information about publishers of all sorts—books, magazine, photograph, greeting card, cartoon—in *Literary Marketplace* and *Writer's Market* (each issued every year). There is a great deal of information in each of these source books. Here, for example, is the *Writer's Market* entry for this publisher:

> **William Kaufmann, Inc.,** One First St., Los Altos CA 94022. Editor-in-Chief: William Kaufmann. Publishes hardcover and paperback originals. Generally offers standard minimum book contract of 10-12.5-15 percent, but special requirements of book may call for lower royalties. No advance. Published 12 titles last year. Query first. Reports

within a few weeks. Enclose S.A.S.E.

Education: Main interests are academic trade books; that is, general interest books that are developed by professional teachers or by well-known writers, and are aimed at readers with good high school or even college education. Prefer books suitable for use as supplemental reading or basic adoption for forward-looking courses; but not particularly interested in conventional textbooks. Good writing, high quality (accuracy and depth), originality, are major qualities sought. Should be for literate, issue or problem oriented audiences, and have staying power (not too ephemeral, trendy, etc.). Originality in approach, format, organization, and illustration. Adult trade fiction, economics, environmental law, politics, regional planning, and scientific areas.

agents

Although few nonfiction writers do so, you can use an agent to market your book for you. He or she will read your manuscript, comment on it, and try to sell it. As agents depend upon commissions (generally 10 percent of the author's royalties), they may be reluctant to accept new clients. A few of them charge a reading fee. As publishers do not charge for reading, there is no reason to use an agent for nonfiction unless you do not wish to be bothered with business, or are unduly disturbed at being rejected. Rejection is no disgrace; some fast-selling books have been rejected by as many as 40 publishers! Agents, too, are listed in *Writer's Market* and *Literary Marketplace.*

letter of inquiry

Once you have decided on a publisher, your best course of action is to write a letter of inquiry—even if your manuscript is essentially complete. It should include a statement of your thesis (what the book is about), a summary of your treatment, an estimate of the size, number, and kind of illustrations, an estimate of the length of the manuscript, and an idea of your intended audience. You should attach an outline and a few pages of text to help the editor and publisher assess your writing style.

Writer's Market recommends that unknown writers include the first two or three chapters, or two or three that the author feels are especially well written or have unusual appeal.

You should give the editor an idea also of who you are so that he can judge whether he is dealing with a professional writer or a professional scientist. Do be brief; if you are a well-known scientist sending a book to a publisher who specializes in your field, he'll know you or be able to find out about you. If you are a writer, your work will speak for itself.

If you are really eminent in your field, the letter of inquiry may be enough. However, modesty is always winning, and the time you spend organizing your thoughts to produce a thorough outline is usually well invested, even if your final product bears little resemblance to your original outline.

"SASE"

Whether you send a letter of inquiry or a full manuscript, be sure to include "SASE" (self-addressed, stamped envelope). Some publishers will not return a manuscript or even reply unless SASE is included in the first round of correspondence. Although most scientific journals and scholarly publishers do not require SASE for simple correspondence, most do require it for large, unsolicited packages. In addition, if you always make a point of including SASE in your initial correspondence with a publisher, you cannot forget to include your address—which writers have been known to do! Do not be discouraged if you do not get a reply by return mail.

contracts

Contracts vary widely. A contract with a subsidy publisher will require you to pay, but a contract with a commercial publisher may give you an *advance*—money the publisher gives you out of your royalties before your book has earned it. The actual amount of royalties ranges from none (as in the case of some scholarly and technical books) to 40 or 50 percent (given by subsidy publishers out of your own money).

Many publishers offer royalties on a sliding scale: the first few thousand copies (while the cost of printing is being paid) at a low percentage, the next few thousand at a higher percentage, and all beyond a certain minimum at a fairly high rate. This allows the author and publisher to share somewhat the financial risks. Royalties may be lower on paperback books, on textbooks, or on such special printings as book-club editions.

Unless you write a best seller, you should not expect to make a lot of money on your book, particularly if the potential audience is small. We've heard of publishers of sexy novels bordering on the pornographic who pay as little as $250 outright for an entire book. Surely in such a case the author must write for the love of the subject!

A scientist who writes on a subject of specialist scope must also write for that reason. He may never receive even $250 for his efforts. In fact, in many cases he may be required to pay "page charges," which we will discuss later.

A good writer can make almost any subject interesting. For example, we recall reading a description of a cold macaroni sandwich that was so enticing our mouths watered for one. Few scientists produce prose of this quality, or have subjects of as wide an appeal as food; they must expect a smaller audience for a restricted subject: therefore, small royalties. Compare contracts and experience with your colleagues who have published. They can give you an idea of the returns you can expect, as well as the anguish involved in production.

Most reputable publishers are as good as their word, and therefore oral contracts should be adequate. However, an editor may not stay at one publisher's office long enough to fulfill the oral contract he made with an author, or the entire publishing firm may be sold. It is wise, for both parties, to have a formal contract in writing.

Beware of contracts that limit your rights as a writer. Some contracts have a clause that would prevent you from writing a competing book. This is reasonable; the publisher wishes to protect his investment. However, you should be sure that this does not limit you so much that it can prevent you from writing in your field.

pricing your book

How much a book costs does not seem like a writer's concern, except when collecting royalties, but the publisher may accept or reject a book on the basis of its ultimate selling price. A general rule is that the retail price is five times the cost of printing. Therefore, if a book costs $2 to print, it must be priced at $10. This allows for advertising, retail and wholesale markup, and the many other costs of publishing. Therefore, the publisher—and the author—must consider the potential market. How many copies will readers buy at $10?

Another way of pricing a book is to consider that question first: How many copies can be sold at $10? How many at $8? If a competing book exists, what is its price? If the competitor is selling for $6, can you produce a book that costs only $1 to print that can be sold for $5? Looking at it from this point of view, the publisher will probably restrict the author to a certain number of pages, and a certain number and kind of illustrations.

For example, we know of an author who produced a superb guidebook to a small but interesting area in the Far West. She purchased photographs from the world's best photographers, solicited and edited contributions from leading experts, and had art work prepared by outstanding artists—all paid for from her own pocket. When the manuscript was complete, the publisher who had expressed interest in it refused to publish it on the ground that the potential audience was too small to repay the heavy cost of printing.

What is the answer? Larger subject? Fewer illustrations? Less thorough coverage? Such a work as a general dictionary, which has very high total production costs, nonetheless has a broad potential audience, which allows the cost per unit to be low. In printing, the initial costs (which include typesetting) are very high; reprinting is far less expensive.

Similarly, a large press run yields a much lower unit cost than a small press run. If you can anticipate selling 100,000 copies of your book quickly, the publisher might be able to print it for as little as 50c each, allowing a selling price of $2.50. If your audience will total only about 1,000 all told, the same book might cost as much as $3 per copy to print, requiring a selling price of $15! These are publication problems that you must be aware of, though you may not deal with them directly.

choosing a title

Choose a title for your book at least as carefully as you would select the given name for your first-born child. In making the choice, work closely with your editor or publisher, who will be concerned with factors perhaps not familiar to you—factors like marketing and advertising.

Try to find a distinctive title, or at least one not close to that of a competing work still in print. If possible your title should be informative; bear in mind the advantages of key words for computer-based bibliographies and for indexing. It should also be easy to refer to in speech, even if in a shortened or casual form.

Generally speaking, you should keep the title short. There is nothing wrong with adding a subtitle even if it is of considerable length. But it may not be wise to strain too hard to make the title fully and accurately reflect the content: *War and Peace* and *The Origin of Species* have done well despite brevity.

Every year hundreds of authors begin their books' titles with *Introduction to,* thereby sentencing them to burial among their fellow *Introductions* in card catalogs and references like *Books in Print.* (check that reference in your bookstore or library to see what we mean.) So, avoid words like *Introduction, General, Beginning,* and *Selected,* at least at the beginning of your title.

Avoid too general terms such as *Botany* and, at the other extreme, the overly recondite such as *Maestrichtian animalculae* unless you are eager to appeal to a very small circle of readers indeed.

magazine articles

Costs and titles are important to publishers of magazines, too. If you write an article for a commercial magazine or newspaper, you may be paid by the word, column, or page, but the length will probably be specified by the publisher. If you are a recognized expert, you may be asked to write a specialized article. In this case, the publisher or editor who asks you for the article will probably indicate the required length. Payment for such work ranges from copies of the magazine or book in which it appears to several thousand dollars for special material. Some publishers pay for illustrations separately; others pay for the entire package as a lump sum.

If you wish to contribute an unsolicited article to a magazine, you have two choices: send the entire article, or preface it with a letter of inquiry. However, you will save yourself trouble, money, and time by becoming familiar with potential markets for your article before sending either a letter or a manuscript to any editor.

matching article and journal

Whether you are writing a technical report for a noncommercial audience or a general article for a large audience, you should match your message to the journal. As editorial policies may change over the years, don't trust your recollection of the magazine. Make a list of potential markets, then obtain a recent copy of each magazine and study it. Many editors will supply a special guide for interested writers, giving their editorial philosophy and requirements. Sometimes, too, they will send a sample copy of their magazine either free or for the price of a single issue.

If you receive a "not interested" reply to your letter of inquiry, then try another magazine on your list. If necessary, reword the letter, tailoring it to the interests of the editor you are now addressing. In any event, retype it. Don't use a duplicated form letter; if you do, you'll probably get a duplicated "no."

In the editorial description of the magazine, you may note "simultaneous submissions considered." This means that you can submit the article to two or more publishers at the same time, if you indicate that you have done so. It is even possible to sell the article twice, if the magazines are not competitive, but that is rare, and in no case should you do it without the knowledge and consent of both editors. Once the article is published, it can be republished with the permission of the copyright owner. Republication, condensation, or alteration to another medium are all matters for negotiation. In any event, depending upon what rights you retained, you should receive some payment for republication and for other versions of your material.

technical papers

The procedure involved in publishing an article in a primary scientific journal is not altogether different. The major differences between commercial periodicals and technical journals are that most technical journals employ the peer review system and few pay the authors for their efforts. In fact, many ask that the author pay. This system, called "page charges," is somewhat flexible. Basically, the author is asked to contribute a certain sum per printed page to help the publisher (generally a learned society) defray expenses.

page charges

The sum varies from publisher to publisher, and may be as much as $100 per printed page. However, the method is not always equally applied. Some publishers ask for page charges if the author has obtained grant funds to pay for publication, or if his employer will pay; an individual is rarely assessed. For example, one publisher has a certain quota of nonpay articles for each issue. Beyond that, this publisher will accept no article, regardless of merit, whose author cannot pay charges. Other publishers admit that the article that can pay its own way has priority over those that cannot. Neither authors nor publishers are comfortable with the system, but the alternative may be far fewer articles published. Recent enforcement by the Postal Service may doom the page-charge system, although a compromise may be worked out.

house style

Scientific journals, even more than books or commercial magazines, require that you conform to house style. The reason is that most journal editors are unpaid, having been appointed or elected to that position, and simply do not have time to copyedit and retype your manuscript. Write for a style sheet from the journal you have in mind, and follow their instructions religiously.

If the journal has no style sheet, study a recent issue, looking carefully at abbreviations, citations, footnotes, abstracts, figures, captions, and text.

Once the editor of a commercial magazine agrees to consider your manuscript, or you have determined which scientific journal you're going to favor with your words, you're ready to write and mail. For advice on writing, see pages 7-16; for instructions on typing, pages 20-22. Write a cover letter stating what you wish the editor to do with the manuscript.

Enclose the letter with the manuscript, along with return postage. Send the manuscript and the letter, well wrapped, to the editor, but do retain a carbon copy. There are special postage rates for manuscript material, but if your package is addressed to a destination within 500 miles, private delivery services may be cheaper and quicker.

peer review

When your manuscript arrives at the editorial offices of a primary journal or a textbook publisher, it may undergo the peer review process. This system, like page charges, is not always equable. Virtually all primary scientific journals and publishers use it as a means of judging the worth of manuscripts, but how effective it is depends in part upon the objectivity of the reviewer and author. Reviewers are generally chosen for their knowledge of the subject matter. Few are paid, except those who act as publisher's advisors for textbooks, but a good reviewer is beyond price. He (or she) can steer an author away from a false conclusion, can suggest related work the author may or may not know of, and may even help clarify difficult wording. However, editing is not the reviewer's job, and a good one tries not to usurp the editor's task, particularly in matters of editorial or typographic style.

This is not the place to discuss reviewing at length, but if you are asked to review a manuscript, try to be constructive in your criticism. A scrawled "this fool doesn't know what he is talking about" across a manuscript means trouble for the editor (who must soothe a wounded author), for the publisher (whose choice of a reviewer may have to be defended), for the author (who must retype that page), and for you (the editor is not likely to speak well of you).

As an author, you may or may not find out who your reviewers have been. Some journals will not reveal the names of reviewers; some reviewers do not wish to have their identities exposed. As a general rule, it is the conscientious, constructive reviewer who is willing to be known.

When you receive reviews, you should suppress your natural defensive reactions toward criticism, leaning instead toward careful consideration of all comments. You surely will learn something, if not about the subject, then about yourself.

If your manuscript was rejected on the basis of comments from a reviewer, and you believe the comments to be unfair, ask the editor to seek another opinion. Often it will be done.

Once you're through the hoops—reviewers, editors, and the publisher have all said "yes"—you're on your way to print. You no longer need market your manuscript; at last you can begin the final steps leading to publication.

digging deeper

Writing to Sell (Scott Meredith, 2nd edition, 1974; Harper & Row, New York) concerns just that: writing and selling what you write, as described by a man who is perhaps the most successful of all literary agents. If you don't use an agent, and possibly even if you do, you should be familiar with two annual guides to the world of magazine and book publishers: *Literary Marketplace* (R.R. Bowker Co., New York) and *Writer's Market* (Writer's Digest, Cincinnati). Each of these annuals is packed with names and addresses of publishers, the kinds of material each publishes, and other pertinent information. *A Writer's Guide to Book Publishing* (1977; Hawthorn Books, New York), written by Richard Balkin, an agent, is particularly valuable for the business end of publishing.

key points

When seeking a publisher

- select one who specializes in your field
- write a letter of inquiry
- follow publisher's style
- use criticism to improve your manuscript

17 PUBLISHING: doing it yourself

"Of the making of many books," the Preacher wrote, "there is no end." There is no shortage of books in the western world, and there need be no end to good ones. The worth of a book is not to be judged by its sales; some very bad books (from several points of view) are best sellers, and some very good ones are never published.

One alternative to not letting a good book languish is for the author to publish it himself. All manner of works are published "privately" in this way, although many of them are offered for public sale. You may have helped to publish your society's newsletter, or a guidebook to your city's architecture or history, or part of your family records.

"Self-publishing" is particularly well suited to works that have a small potential audience. This is not to say that there are not occasional surprises. For example, writer-psychologist Freda Morris sold her book on self-hypnosis to a major publisher only after her self-published edition had attracted widespread interest. (In her article in the magazine *The Self-Publishing Writer,* she called major publishers "the enemy.") Dr. Morris received a $5,000 advance royalty payment for the book and also gained the publisher's interest in her future work. The first printing of the commercial edition was 20,000, which is a much larger number than usual.

Mark Twain's *Huckleberry Finn* was originally a self-published work, and since the first edition it has sold millions of copies. Many other authors, now prominent, launched their careers with their own editions; among them are Thomas Paine, William Blake, Percy Bysshe Shelley, Washington Irving, Stephen Crane, Upton Sinclair, Zane Grey, and Carl Sandburg. General H.M. Roberts self-published his *Pocket Manual of Rules of Order for Deliberative Assemblies.* More recently, Anais Nin attained nationwide fame with a 300-copy edition of *Winter of Artifice.* And *The Whole Earth Catalog,* a self-published, self-distributed venture, won the National Book Award.

American scientists of last century were likely to be author, artist, publisher, and salesman rolled into one. Ornithologist Alexander Wilson sold his work door-to-door by subscription, the proceeds of each volume being used to pay the printing costs of the next.

Many scientists, even today, are "self-publishers" for what amounts to the first edition of their work. When they issue a "preprint" or an "open-file" edition of a scientific paper, they are, in effect, publishing it themselves.

If you do decide to publish the work yourself, you have several options: 1) you can contract with a subsidy publisher; 2) you can ask a printer to print the book for you from your manuscript copy; 3) you can prepare it and print it yourself; 4) you can prepare camera-ready copy for a printer to print.

subsidy publishers

Although many printers will publish books paid for by the author, some publishing houses, called subsidy or "vanity" presses, specialize in this form of publication. They will edit, print, and distribute your work, but you must pay for it. Subsidy publishers agree to a much larger royalty rate than commercial firms, but they rarely have salesmen, and they advertise and promote the book only minimally. You cannot often expect to make money from a subsidy-published venture.

Reputable subsidy publishers will offer clear contracts and will live up to their agreements. Beware of fly-by-night publishers who may never deliver even one printed book. For a list of reputable subsidy presses see *Writer's Market.*

publishing with a printer

If you decide to go to a printer, he will help you with all the publishing details, but he may or may not wish to help you with distribution of the completed book. In any event, if you choose this route, you will be called upon to make decisions as to format, style and size of type, arrangement of illustrations and text, kind of paper, type of binding, and other matters. The printer will follow your instructions, and will deliver to you a supply of nicely bound books and a bill for his services.

In many ways, this is the easiest route, as you are able to participate in all decisions and will have a professionally printed book as a product. It is up to you to see that the book is professionally written, professionally illustrated, professionally edited, professionally designed and professionally proofed.

All of the publisher's other tasks—obtaining the ISBN number, registering the copyright, etc.—will also fall on you. Check the list on pages 103-104 to make certain that you forget nothing that should be included in the printed volume.

printing it yourself

The third method—you do it all—is the tried-and-true method for small school newspapers, club newsletters, and the like. "Do-it yourself" printing ranges from the complete home workshop for fine printing to pencil and carbon paper. Some people who make a hobby of fine printing have their own print shop at home, and take great pride in producing superb work. We have one friend who makes her own paper, designs her own type, and prints her own (very small) books. If you are knowledgeable enough to design your own type, you probably don't need any advice from us!

spirit duplicating

For a small number of copies, or if your budget is miniscule, you may want to print the book yourself on some type of copying machine. If you have a spirit duplicator, you can write or draw on spirit masters ("Ditto" is one brand of these) and print in one or more colors. This method is very inexpensive and very messy. Copies do fade with time.

ink-master printing

Nearly as cheap and almost as messy, but more permanent, is the ink-master system, which uses masters that require you to cut out letters and lines by typewritter or stylus ("Mimeograph" is a brand name).

electrostatic copying

Use of both the spirit-master and the ink-master system has declined in recent years as photocopying and electrostatic copying has increased. Each is a far cleaner method to use than the master system. Modern copy machines can use virtually anything that will fit on the glass carrier as a master, although some colors, lines, and originals reproduce better than others.

Electrostatic copying ("Xerox" is one brand) is easy, neat, and the image lasts. It is, however, fairly expensive. For short runs (meaning a few copies), this may not be critical.

Electrostatic copying is similar to offset printing in that "what you see is what you get," but it differs in that offset printing can reproduce illustrations handsomely, and can reproduce many copies quickly and inexpensively. If you plan to print a substantial number of copies—say, more than 100—offset printing is the path to choose.

offset printing

To prepare material for offset (assuming that you plan to do it all except prepare the printing negatives and plates and do the actual printing), you will need to set copy, organize illustrations, and dummy your book.

You can set copy in one of many ways. One friend of ours, Ralph Rambo, uses pen and india ink to produce charmingly illustrated books, maps, and drawings. A page from one of his books is shown in Figure 29. All his words are lettered by hand, so that each page is treated as if it were an illustration. When President Gerald Ford visited San Jose (Mr. Rambo's home town in California) a copy of some of Mr. Rambo's drawings and an introduction to him were highlights of the presidential visit!

Most people will not want to take the time to hand letter their own books; indeed, few of us could. An alternative to this is to use a typewriter equipped with carbon ribbon. Cloth ribbon will not do. Some modern electric typewriters not only give an even impression, but are also equipped with devices that will allow you to make even right-hand ("justified") margins, and to select any of several book-style type faces.

justifying

Years before such machines were readily available, one of us published several books with justified right-hand margins. We justified them by typing each line as close to, but short of, the desired length as possible, then counting the number of letters needed to justify the line. Then, retyping each paragraph or page, we inserted extra spaces judiciously here and there so that the double spacing did not show. At times, when a line would not justify without leaving obvious gaps, we rewrote the line.

Modern electric typewriters have all manner of aids for the self-publisher. It is possible to rent or lease magnetic card ("mag-card") typewriters, which will reproduce what you type over and over again without your retyping it. You can leave room to type in addresses, you can insert new paragraphs, or you can make corrections that the typewriter will type automatically.

Or, you can type on an electric typewriter using a particular font ("ball") and a set of special symbols that

DESPITE PAST SHATTERED INDUSTRIAL DREAMS, ALVISO WAS LIVELY. THE INFAMOUS 1896 "NEW CHICAGO" LAND PROMOTION, THE VALLEY'S EARLY "SUBDIVISION", BY THIS TIME WAS ALMOST FORGOTTEN. JAMES LICK'S MAHOGANY FLOUR MILL WAS CLOSED AS WAS THE SAN JOSE WATCH FACTORY THAT MADE ONLY A FEW TIMEPIECES. BUT ORTLEY'S MILL WAS GRINDING ITS ENDLESS SUPPLY OF OYSTER SHELLS FOR POULTRY USES. THE FERTILE VALLEY'S PRODUCTS WERE STEADILY FILLING THE ALVISO WHARVES AND WAREHOUSES WITH STACKS OF PRODUCE, BALED HAY, GRAIN AND DRIED FRUIT. LONG FLAT BARGES WERE BEING LOADED WITH MOUNTAINOUS PILES OF SACKED POTATOES AND ONIONS.

IT WAS TOO EARLY FOR US TO SEE MR. WELCH, "THE MAN WHO ALWAYS DROVE AN EMPTY WAGON." DRAWN BY A STRAINING TEAM OF FOUR HORSES, NO LOAD WAS EVER VISIBLE. THE WAGON BOTTOM CONTAINED MAXIMUM HAULING WEIGHT; ONE LAYER OF IRON FLASKS, EACH FILLED WITH 76 POUNDS OF QUICKSILVER FROM THE ALMADEN MINES AND BOUND FOR PORTS OF THE WORLD.

WE TURNED INTO A NARROW LANE SNAKING ITS WAY AROUND THE INLETS AND BAYOUS OF THE ALVISO SLOUGH INTO A STRANGE AND DIFFERENT WORLD. I CLUNG TO ELVIRA AS WE SWAYED PRECARIOUSLY; THE BUGGY WHEELS OFTEN SINKING TO THE HUBS IN TREACHEROUS HOLES AND BLUE MUD. AROUND US WERE SWARMS OF WILD FOWL, DUCKS, GEESE, SNIPE, KILLDEER AND RED-WING BLACKBIRDS. FLOCKS OF TINY SHORE BIRDS SKIMMED OR PARADED THE SHINY MUD FLATS. ONE BIRD OVERWHELMED ALL OTHERS IN NUMBERS,— THE MUD HEN. TO ME IT SEEMED THERE WERE MILLIONS OF THESE SLEEK BLUE-GRAY WATER FOWL BUSILY SWIMMING, MUD-SCRATCHING, DIVING, CLUCKING.

CONVERSATION HAD LAGGED UP TO THIS POINT BUT NOW THE SUN WARMED US AND WE WERE NEARING OUR OBJECTIVE. SO I BROUGHT UP THE SUBJECT OF MUD HENS.

"ARE THEY GOOD TO EAT AS OTHER DUCKS, MR. CYRUS?" I ASKED.

HE FAVORED ME WITH A LOOK OF TOLERANT PITY. "THEY AINT DUCKS, BUD; NOT EVEN RELATED. THEY BELONGS TO THE SNIPE FAMILY. TAKE NOTICE THAT THEIR TOES AINT WEBBED LIKE A DUCK'S? TO BE TETNICAL, ACTUAL THEY'RE COOTS."

I STRAINED OUT ANOTHER BRILLIANT QUERY, "WHY ARE THEY CALLED MUD HENS?"

"I DON'T KNOW EXACT, BUD," HE ADMITTED BEFORE QUICKLY COOKING UP AN ANSWER, "RECKON THERE'S SO MANY OF 'EM, FEED GETS SCARCE. SO THEY JIST EAT MUD, HOPIN' SOMETHIN' WORTH WHILE WILL SIFT OR STRAIN INTO 'EM. THAT MAKES 'EM MUD HENS.

25

Page from *Me and Cy,* a hand-lettered, hand-drawn book published by the author, Ralph Rambo. FIGURE 29 constitute instructions to a typesetting machine. Your typed copy can then be given to an optical character recognition (OCR) machine, which will "read" the copy, follow the instructions you have provided, and return to you typeset, justified copy ready to be given to the printer for photographing directly.

pasting up

If you do not elect to do the actual typing yourself, you can give your text to a printer to have it set in hot or cold type (see page 129). You can use the copy from the printer to paste up pages exactly as you would like them to be printed. Remember—whether you get copy from the printer or set it yourself—that you may be pasting up the only typeset copy of your work. If you allow errors in typesetting to remain, arrange the material in the wrong order, paste it up crooked, or get it smudged or dirty, that is the way it will be printed.

correcting errors

Errors do creep in, of course. The trick is to find them before you go to press. Proofread everything carefully, then reproof it. If you are having your book set in hot type, or if someone is setting cold type for you, indicate your corrections as shown on pages 133-138. Whether you set the type yourself or ask someone else to, you, as the publisher, are the only one who will be hunting for errors. Get friends to help you proof it, but don't let them handle the one and only copy of cold-type composition. If you've typed it yourself, you'll know why. Protect the original with a plastic cover, and never, never write on it. Better yet, make electrostatic copies of the original typeset material and proofread them. Copies can be smudged, corrected, erased, drawn on, or destroyed and no harm is done. Use the original only to make actual corrections.

Make your corrections (or have them made) before "pasting up"; it is very difficult to make corrections in pasted-up copy. You can make corrections by resetting the line, paragraph, or page. Or, if you have a correction as small as a word or a letter that will occupy the same space as the error, you can do this: using a light-table, place the correction over the original in the exact position you want the correction to appear. With a very sharp artist's knife or a sharp, single-edge razor blade, cut through both sheets around the correction, being careful not to cut through any words.

Do not let the knife cut any letter except the incorrect one. Throw away the cut-out error. Carefully remove the correction and lay that to one side. Place a piece of transparent tape on the back of your typeset copy, over the hole where the error was removed. Very carefully place the correction in the hole so that it fits perfectly and is held in by the tape. (We have always used a dissecting needle for this.) When through, you should have only a faint line around the correction, which must be removed by opaquing paint on the printer's negative.

dummying

So far, we've been mentioning "paste-up" and "dummy" without telling you what these mean. You or your printer will make a "layout," which is a mock-up of each page, to show exactly how the type and illustrations will be arranged. A good layout requires knowledge of good design, which is beyond the scope of this book. However, the references at the end of this chapter and on page 131 will help you. Try to design your book so that it is an esthetically unified whole, then design each two facing pages as units.

When the whole book is arranged in this way, you have made a "dummy." From the dummy, make a "paste-up," if the book is to be printed by an offset method. The paste-up consists of the actual type to be photographed by the printer fastened in the exact position you wish it to appear. Pasting up is detailed work, requiring a good eye for straightness, a good memory for parts, and compulsive neatness.

To make a paste-up, you will need blank sheets showing the dimensions of each page and the margin area. If the blank sheets are larger than the finished book, you will have room outside the margins to make notes to the printer (see Figure 30).

Using rubber cement, hot wax, or invisible mending tape in the corners only (do not use cellophane tape), fasten each piece of copy *exactly* where you want it to be, leaving space for illustrations. Place the captions in their spots, too, but do *not* paste in the illustrations. Remember to include the "running heads"—the identification of the book—(if you want them), and, surely, the page numbers. Any special instructions you may have for the printer can be written outside the margin (not in the margin). It is wise to have at hand a pencil with non-photographic blue lead. These are available at art stores.

Each piece of art work should be clearly marked for amount of reduction, placement (page and position), top, and number of parts. (See pages 50-53.) You also need to indicate the screen you would like used on the halftone illustrations. If you don't understand halftone screens, consult your printer.

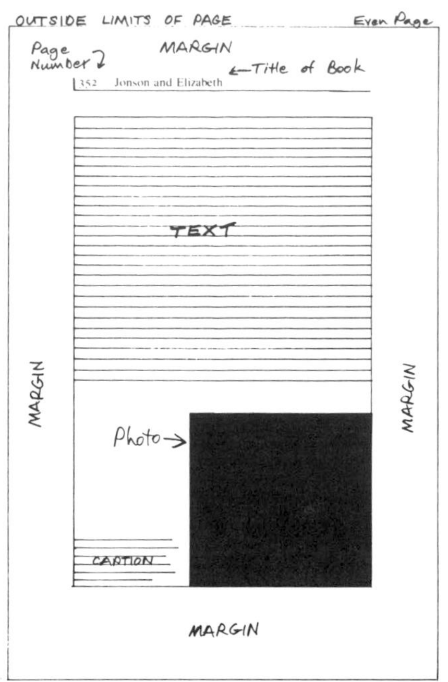

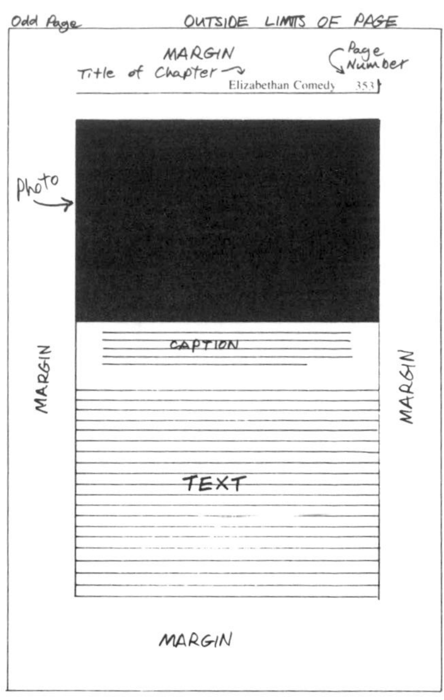

FIGURE 30 Dummy sheets to be used for layout (stickup) should be made to show the exact size of your final book page. Mark the outside limits of text in non-photographic blue. Remember to leave room for page numbers and (if you wish) the title of the book and chapter at the top or bottom. Paste the text and captions on the sheet absolutely straight and even. Mark limits (size) of illustrations—final size, that is, the size that will be printed—but do not fasten them down with the text.

Pages that open chapters, have headings, or illustrations that extend beyond the margin will be different.

When you have finished pasting up your book, take the entire copy, together with illustrations, to the printer. Although pasting pages in the arrangement they will have in each "signature" (group of pages printed together) is possible, it rarely saves time. The exact arrangement depends upon the number of pages in the book, the size and kind of press to be used to print it, the size of copy camera available, and other factors beyond your control. Regardless of the arrangement of pages for the press, the pages will appear in consecutive order in the book.

Your illustrations, carefully identified (see pages 50-53), must be given to the printer in finished form. If you are publishing the book yourself, you must be your own art director, as well as designer and editor.

binding After the book is printed, no matter how you do it, you will want to have it bound. You may already have chosen the binding method. If it is a short book (fewer than 100 pages), your printer probably will suggest "saddle-stitching," which is simply a method of holding the book together by fasteners—such as staples—down the center.

Longer books are usually gathered—that is, the signatures are stacked in order and the book stitched along the edge using thread or wire. Gathered books can be bound in cloth, plastic, or leather, or can be glued to paper or plastic covers. Many paperback books are "perfect" bound. In perfect binding, the stacked signatures are trimmed and glued to the binding. This kind of binding is less expensive but also less durable than stitched bindings.

If you have produced your own book sheet by sheet on a copying machine, there are several options for binding. You can have the copies perfect bound in a good cover if you wish, you can staple it yourself, or have it bound in any one of several kinds of spiral or patent bindings. Spiral bindings are especially good for field books and guide books, as well as cookbooks and other books of instructions that must lie flat. Another alternative is a loose-leaf book, in which you provide pages with or without binders. Many firms publish loose-leaf catalogs so that pages can easily be changed.

The largest part of the cost of any cover is the art work on it, the material you use for it, and the cost of printing it. "Self-cover," that is, covers made of the same paper as the book itself, are cheapest; leather the most expensive.

As for the actual bindery work, the cost of punching holes in the paper for a loose-leaf binder and the cost of stapling are about equal; both are very small. Spiral and perfect bindings cost a little more. Stitched, gathered bindings (such as those used on "hard cover" books) are more costly.

costs How much will it all cost? There are various arrangements with printers and subsidy presses to provide help in marketing your book. In general, however, it all comes down to your paying the printing bill. Subsidy presses expect you to pay; for this, they will give you copies of your book and very high (45%) royalty on your books that they sell. Other printers have different contract arrangements. One printer lists nine ways to publish a book with him, all but one of which require the author to pay all costs.

Prices are rising so rapidly today that it is difficult to

give figures as to how much any book will cost. Take these estimates as educated guesses for 1977 printing prices at an inexpensive press, which has set your book in cold type and printed it by offset methods:

Number of pages	Number of copies		
	500	1000	10,000
64	$800 ($1.60 each)	$1100 ($1.10 each)	$7000 ($.70 each)
128	$1600 ($3.20 each)	$2200 ($2.20 each)	$14,000 ($1.40 each)
320	$4000 ($8.00 each)	$5500 ($5.50 each)	$35,000 ($3.50 each)

We emphasize that these are *printing* costs. Even if we ignore the time you spend, you will still have art and photography costs, research costs, advertising costs, and distribution costs. You may also be required to have a business license and a tax permit.

distributing your book

How will you recoup? If you are publishing for the members of an organization, recovering your costs may be more or less guaranteed. If not, you must make your book known to prospective purchasers. You can do this by word-of-mouth, by sales in stores, by advertising, by reviews, by selling at fairs and shows, by appearing on talk shows, or by any other method you can think of.

digging deeper

Ten years ago almost no information on "small" or do-it-yourself publishing was available except advertisements for subsidy publishers. Today, the independent, almost-noncommercial publisher is a growing phenomenon, particularly for art and literary books. There is even a journal entitled *The Self-Publishing Writer* (P.O. Box 24, San Francisco), which contains articles on self-publishing experiences and some help for self publishers.

Personal experiences in do-it-yourself publishing, including those of such notables as Anais Nin, Leonard Woolf, Oliver Lange, Stewart Brand, and Alan Swallow, among others, are contained in *The Publish-It-Yourself-Handbook* (1973; Pushcart Book Press, P.O. Box 845, Yonkers, New York).

Two pamphlets by printers include Hawkes Publishing Company's *How to Get Your Book Published; Answers to Questions That Authors Have for Publishers* (P.O. Box 15711, Salt Lake City) and Robert Olmsted's *The Neat Nine; 9 Ways To Be an Author* (Northwoods Press, P.O. Box 24, Bigfork, Minnesota). Bear in mind that the ways have you pay the bills.

Help in the actual offset printing process may be obtained in *Printing It,* by Clifford Burke (1972; Wingbow Press, Berkeley, California); first aid for problems in selling it can be obtained from *Promotion* (1975; Committee of Small Magazine Editors and Publishers, P.O. Box 703, San Francisco).

The entire publication process is covered in *How to Publish Your Own Book* (1976; Harlo Press, Detroit). It is also detailed in *How to Self-Publish Your Own Book & Make It a Best Seller!* (1975; Enterprise Publishing Company, 1300 Market St. Wilmington, Delaware), but the emphasis is on promotion.

Self publishing has become so respectable and prevalent in recent years that a major "slick" magazine has published an article entitled "The pleasures and perils of self-publishing," by Mary Anne Guitar *(Mademoiselle,* November, 1975).

One Book/Five Ways (1978; William Kaufmann, Inc., Los Altos, California) is an enlightening peek into the publishing world. Do-it-yourselfers will find considerable food for thought in these five case histories. Each case history is the life story of a proposed trade book, entitled "No Time for House Plants", from manuscript to printed form. *One Book/Five Ways* shows how five different university presses (University of Chicago Press, MIT Press, University of North Carolina Press, University of Texas Press, and University of Toronto Press) would have produced the book. *One Book/Five Ways* reproduces all the correspondence with the author of "No Time for House Plants": the budget, plans for production, layouts, prospective sales campaign, and other details of the publication route for each of the five different presses involved. It shows that there is "more than one way to make a book."

key points

Publish your work yourself if you are willing to

- pay the expense
- take the time
- undertake distribution

18 PRINTING: working with editor and publisher

After you've found a publisher, or a publisher has found you, you enter a difficult but stimulating phase of seeing your work into print. You will work with specialists in fields much different from your own, and sometimes the book will seem more theirs than yours. But now their role is equally important, and at the least you should find publication much more familiar and even easier the next time around.

publishers and editors

In many places in this book, we speak of "publisher" and "editor" as if they were different persons, but often that is not so—the publisher may merely change hats, shifting from one job function to another. However it happens to be in your case, once you and the publisher have agreed on a contract the editor takes over, and much depends on what kind of an editor you have. (The editor might prefer to say that much depends on what kind of an author you are.)

kinds of editors

Editors vary. Some are passive and will merely guide your work into print; this kind may allow you to make errors without warning you. Some will be dictatorial and all but rewrite your work for you. Others (the best, in our view) will bombard you with queries, suggestions, alternatives, advice, and pertinent information, and even (let's hope) may have the experience and judgment to know when to let you have your own way and when to overrule you.

Do your best to determine what kind of editor you have, and adapt as well as you can. The potential for friction is great, but so is the potential for achievement.

Your editor will be much concerned with the production schedule—that is, with coordinating the flow of copy (your typescript) to the typesetter; galley proofs from typesetter to editor and to you; corrected galleys to the editor and to you; reproduction proofs and art work to the printer; page proofs from printer to editor and you; corrected page proofs back to the printer; and, at last, bluelines and corrected bluelines. The schedule will include printing and binding, too, but those will not involve you directly.

working with your editor

You are more likely to be conscious of your editor as a copyeditor than as a production specialist. A good one will overwhelm you with queries and suggestions: You have written "a number of specimens"; don't you know how many? You say "in 1906 in San Francisco," thereby stressing the place, but in the rest of the paragraph you are stressing the time instead of the place, and so you should make it "in San Francisco in 1906." Your quotation on page 36 doesn't read smoothly; please check your source. Have you obtained permission to reproduce Figure 8-30 from *The Third Planet*? The statement about Stoppard's philosophy on page 59 seems to contradict your quotation on page 33; please reconcile. And so on.

Of course you should have anticipated such queries while rewriting, but like all authors you will reach the limit of your capacity to criticize your own work.

copyediting

Some people spend their entire professional lives in copyediting. Most likely you will spend very little of your life in that work, but the more time you spend on it the more polished your writing will be.

Some copyeditors do little more than watch for the most obvious errors and make sure that your manuscript conforms to the publisher's house style. Many do a great deal more, juggling matters of spelling, punctuation, capitalization, abbreviation, grammar, syntax, English usage, readability, reader level, libel, permissions, cross-references, repetition, plagiarism, logic, and on and on.

A good copyeditor will mark copy neatly for the typesetter, correct some errors and query you on others, point out the problems that only you can solve, help you economize on words, smooth your sentences, and increase the readability of your prose—all the while leaving intact your personal style.

Even if you have the best of copyeditors you should take up the craft yourself and apply it to your own work as an essential part of rewriting. At first you may have to go through your manuscript repeatedly, limiting yourself to a few kinds of problems for each time. Also, you may realize part way through that you've not been consistently spelling 'style book' as two words (or is it one?)—and so you have to start again at the beginning.

production schedule

Some production schedules will not call for all those steps; many will call for more; all will have deadlines. And if anyone misses any one deadline there may be a domino effect on all the others.

Typesetting and printing make up a sophisticated technology, and your editor must keep your manuscript within certain limits (always considering cost as well as feasibility). On the other hand, your editor may open up possibilities you hadn't thought of. Will your halftones reproduce with adequate resolution? Can you use a four-color photo here, or must it be converted to black and white? Is there a more effective way of graphing that information? Your editor can tell you.

design

You may suggest a layout and design for your book, but probably you will not be able to determine it. Among other things, the exact length of your typescript may be a crucial factor in fixing the page size or the number of pages in the finished book. For that reason and others, design of your book may begin only about the time copyediting ends. Some books, especially those in a series, are designed first, and author and editor must work within a specified type-page size and a fixed number of pages and so must produce a text just long enough to fit those specifications.

The length of your typescript is the most obvious factor affecting design. Among the many others are the typeface chosen for the body type; the size of the type; the amount of space (leading) between the lines; the length of the lines (the measure); the size of the margin at the head of the page and at the foot and the sides; the amount of space allotted at the head of each chapter (sinkage); whether or not all chapters must begin on right-hand pages; subheads or other typographic devices used to break up pages of "solid" type; the size and placement of running heads and page numbers . . .

typography

Typography (although probably not your special field) fascinates almost everyone. In fact, when editors first discover the enormous variety of typefaces available they often suffer a sort of design intoxication. However, most soon learn that economy and taste both prevent use of a wide variety of faces on the same page or in the same publication. As the architect Marcel Breuer put it, "Less is more."

typesetting—hot and cold

Only a few years ago, your book almost certainly would have been set in hot type—that is, each letter or other character would have been cast in molten metal. Then (again most likely) the raised surfaces of the type metal would have been inked and pressed against paper—much like printing your name and address with a rubber stamp.

Today your words are more likely to be set by phototypesetting, a process in which each letter is projected (like a miniature slide show) onto photographic film. The product is often called "cold type." By another photographic process, the image of your words will be engraved on a thin metal plate, and the plate will transfer the ink to the paper.

halftones and line work

In any case the photoengraving process will apply to your halftones, which are photographs (and sometimes other art work) that include tones of gray as well as the extremes of black and white. ("Line work" consists of black and white only—no grays—as in line drawings. But note that type, which is solid black, also qualifies as line work.)

All halftones are screened for printing, as you can see by examining photographs in any newspaper (whose coarse screen will be visible to your unaided eye) or book (whose finer screen may force you to use a low-power magnifying glass in order to see it). In color printing, a blue dot produces blue; a blue dot overlapping a yellow dot produces green.

In normal black-and-white printing, an area with no dots appears white, small dots produce gray, and larger dots a darker gray. The size of each dot depends on the amount of light projected through its part of the photo film and thence through the screen (in theory even an ordinary window screen would do), with the chemical solution activated by the light and therefore etching brighter areas more strongly than darker areas.

To print in black and white, the printer puts black ink on white paper. To print in full color is far more complicated and far more expensive: the printer adds first one color of ink and then another, and another . . . One common sequence is yellow, red, blue, and black, each color requiring a separate pass through a press, or a part of a press, and each color being superimposed in exact register on the preceding one.

One of the most expensive aspects of color printing begins long before the presswork begins. That is called "making separations"—that is, separating the component colors from the original photograph and producing a negative for each exactly in register with the other color negatives. These negatives are then used to make the printing plates.

checking illustrations

By the time you receive proof of the illustrations, the printing process will be well under way. You will not be able to make extensive changes at this point. You already have checked and rechecked your data, checked and rechecked spelling, patterns, organization, and all the myriad details in each illustration. You should check it all, one more time, for major errors. What you do about them at this point is moot. Some authors, realizing that their facts are wrongly interpreted, have abandoned publication. You won't let that happen to you.

Assuming that you have done your earlier proofing correctly, what you should pay close heed to now is positioning, patterning, size, and captioning. Ask these questions as you check each illustration: Is this the correct illustration? Is it numbered correctly? Is it in the proper place? Is it in consecutive order with the other illustrations? Is the caption correct? Is it properly worded and spelled? Does it fit the illustration? Is the scale given correctly? (Pay particular attention to this if there has been enlargement or reduction of your original.) Is the illustration right side up? Are all overlays present and in proper register? (Check color photographs as well as art work for registration.) Have any lettering or lines on the illustration been lost or blocked out in the printing process? Is the illustration sharp and clear? Are there extra marks—smudges, ink, dust? Are patterns correct? Have parts of them been lost?

bluelines

Bluelines—usually resembling architectural blueprints—may or may not come to your attention. (Actually you may get brownlines, whitelines, or diazo prints, or others.) This is your last chance: Is the text complete? Are the photos right side up? Are all the headings in place? Are the paragraphs in the right order? Do captions and photos correspond? Does each page number on the contents page lead the reader to the right place?

digging deeper

The best introduction to the whole business of bookmaking is *Bookmaking: The Illustrated Guide to Design and Production* (Marshall Lee, 1965; R.R. Bowker Co., New York). It covers the entire process clearly and in considerable detail. For a brief introduction to typography, see *Typography: Basic Principles* (John Lewis, 1964; Reinhold, New York). For an inexpensive, handy, and throughly sound guide to graphic-arts production, see *Pocket Pal* (11th edition, 1974; International Paper Company, New York).

key points

Once you've found a publisher

- work closely with your editor
- keep in mind design, typesetting, line art, half-tones, and the special demands of color
- check each illustration carefully
- use the blueline to check again

19 PROOFING: copyediting and proofreading

Reading proof is a joy, a temptation, and a burden. It's your first look at your words in type, and a sign that the ordeal is coming to an end. It's a temptation to make expensive changes. And it's hard, exacting work.

galley and page proofs

You may see only the first galley proofs—that is, proofs of the type as it appears before being assembled into pages. You may see also the corrected galleys, then page proofs, and perhaps corrected pages and even bluelines. Keep in mind that at each stage you are closer to the final product, and that at each successive stage errors are easier to see and more expensive to correct.

If you and your editor have done all your work perfectly so far, you will not find it necessary to make changes—the author's alterations or "AAs" that add up so rapidly on the bill for typesetting. However, AAs are always with us, and usually our best hope is to hold them to a minimum.

You may find in the galleys that you have inadvertently plagiarized someone, or made a major error of fact, or that important new information should be added. By all means set the matter aright. But do not fall easily into temptation, and do try to change as few words or lines as possible. Try, too, to make the new version exactly the same length as the old in page proofs; particularly avoid any change that might force a line from one page to another.

When you read the corrected proofs, make certain that the typesetter made exactly the correction specified at each point, and that no new error has been introduced. It is a sound rule to start reading at least three lines above a correction, and to read on to at least three lines below it.

As you proof lines set in hot type, often you can tell which lines were reset by the linotypist, as they may appear to be lighter in color than the uncorrected part. Such lines have been inked but once, whereas the rest of the copy has had two inkings or more, making it print darker.

Cold type, on the other hand, may require an entire paragraph to be reset in order to make corrections. When checking cold type, it is wise to check all of any paragraph that has had corrections made.

If your book is being set by machine (such as by Optical Character Recognition machines), check all the copy, whether or not portions of it required correcting. Machines sometimes introduce errors in copy where none existed before, even though the master has not been altered.

marking proofs

If a friend or colleague also reads your proofs (and the more proofreaders the better), each should use a different color pencil and initial the proofs as they are read.

In marking proofs you must use a special language aiming always at absolute clarity. If the typesetter *can* misunderstand your intention you are risking too much. Make it clear.

As you will see on the next few pages, copyediting symbols and proofreading symbols are largely the same. However, in copyediting the change is made exactly where needed; in proofreading there are usually two marks—one to show where a change is to be made and another in the margin specifying the change.

COPYEDITING SYMBOLS

comma	Standard symbols,when used wisely,help the type-
semicolon	setter; others, too. It may help to remember this
colon	quotation:
quotation mark	Type is set "letter by letter and space by space," so
apostrophe	each letter or space must be clear. Don't forget.
hyphen	Well-edited copy is marked to show the length of

1-em dash	each dash as in this example: the printer Johann
1-en dash	Gutenberg, 1400-1468.
question mark	Doesn't that seem logical
exclamation point	Of course
parentheses	Parentheses as in this example are often necessary;
brackets	brackets editor's notes are somewhat less common,
braces	and braces like these are rarer still.
delete	Editors must mark deletions precisely to prevent
delete, close up to normal	error, bearing mindxx that someone must decide what
delete, close up entirely	to do with the spaace left over.
reduce space	Spacing can be wrong in several ways: here too
add space	much, heretoolittle, and in the next line it is
even spacing	both irregular and uneven as yousee.
add space	Sometimes the spacing between lines is too little;
close up	sometimes it is too much.
indent	Indicate paragraph indentation where necessary.
flush	Or show that you don't want normal indentation.
	If there can be any doubt, mark it "flush".
run in	Or "run in" if that is appropriate.
start new line	You can do this: Start a new line.
run over	You can ask for a letter (or letters) to be run o-
	ver to the next line, or to be run back to the pr
run back	eceding line.
1-em indent	Indentations can be marked like this.
2-em indent	Or this.
flush left	This way for flush left,
flush right	this for flush right,

center	and this for center.
align type	Sometimes type is un ven e and should be marked.
ragged right	You can ask for a ragged margin (mark with a wavy
transpose letters	line). Sometimes letters are tranpsosed, or the word
transpose words	order wrong is. Complicated transpositions can be
followed numbered order	marked as in "letters and words".
author, please clarify	If only the author can clarify a point (does he
auth?	really mean to spell it Psmith?), ask him.
	It is customary to circle figures and words, as in
7; seven	seven and 7, if you mean "do the opposite" -- but
	circling also means "do not set" as in the next
	paragraph.
	Marking type specifications calls for both brevity
	and accuracy; it takes too long to write "Set in
9/11 opt. x 26	9-point Optima, on an 11-point slug, 26 picas wide".
	The most common form of a typeface is called
roman	(sometimes inaccurately) roman. rom
boldface	Boldface is used for sideheads in this book. Scien-
italic	tific names are set in italic, as Atrypa reticularis.
SMALL CAPS	Other special uses call for small capitals, as here;
CAPS AND SMALL CAPS	capitals and small capitals (referred to as "caps
BOLD CAPS	and small caps") and for bold caps. BC
lower case	Capitals Can Be Marked to be set in lower case,
CAPITALS	lower case can be marked for capitals, and so on.
superscript; subscript	Subscripts and superscripts, as in $^{14}C_2$, should be
	marked clearly, as should anything that the typesetter

	might take to be an error (such as the time term
	Polo
this is no error	Recent).
	Finally, use an end mark to show where to stop.
end	30

PROOFREADING SYMBOLS

meaning	marginal symbol	mark in type
insert comma	^,	Standard symbols^ used wisely^ aid the
insert semicolon	^;	typesetter^ others too. A good rule to re-
insert colon	^:	member^ type is set letter by letter and
insert quotation marks	V"	^space by space^ and so each letter and
insert apostrophe	V'	space must be absolutely clear. It won^t do to be ambiguous.
insert hyphen	=	Well^edited copy is marked to show
insert 1-em dash	1/m	the length of each dash^ as in the life
insert 1-en dash	1/n	span of the printer Gutenberg, 1400—^ 1468.
insert question mark	?	Doesn't that approach seem logical^
insert exclamation point	!	Of course^
insert parentheses	( )	Parentheses^ as in this example^ are
insert brackets	[ ]	often needed; brackets^ editor's note^ are
insert braces	{ }	less common. Braces^ like this^ are rarer still.
delete, reduce space		Editors must mark deletions/ pre-
delete, close up entirely		cisely, bearing in mind that some/one must decide what to do with
reduce spaces	⌒	any ^ space ^ left ^ over.
equalize spaces	=#	The^spacing ^ can be ^ wrong ^ in many ways and
add space between words	#	so the instructions by the editorsmust
add space between lines	#	be precise. >Spacing between lines must be changed sometimes, and often a deleted word
restore deleted matter	be	must^ restored.
use normal paragraph indent	¶	^Indicate paragraph indentation where necessary.
do not indent		//←Or show that you don't want the normal indentation.
do not indent	(flush)	// If there can be doubt, mark "flush". Or
no new paragraph; run in	(no ¶)	"run in" if appropriate.
start new line		You can do this: start a new line.
run over to the next line	(run over)	You can run a letter or letters o- ver to the next line, or back to the pr-
run back to previous line	(run back)	eceeding line.

indent 1 em
indent 2 ems
set flush left
set flush right
center
straighten type
push up
push down

align type

turn to proper orientation

with ragged left margin
transpose to order marked
transpose words
transpose letters

author, please clarify

missing copy

use figure, not word,
and vice versa
spell out (or abbreviate)

set in 9-point Optima on an
11-point slug, 26 picas wide
change to roman type
set in bold face

set in italic
set in small caps
set in caps and small caps
set in bold caps
change to lower case
change to upper case
change to proper face
and size
reset broken type

Indentations may be marked like this and this.

This way for flush left,
this for flush right,
and this for center.

Sometimes type is set unevenly and then lines must be reset to straighten the letters or words.

Crooked margins must be aligned in page proofs (it doesn't usually matter in galley proofs). And sometimes a letter is set upside pown.

Ragged margins may be set this way for
effect, with the wavy line properly
marked for instructions.

Sometimes words and letters are transposed, but marking clear will aid correction.

If only the author can answer a question—as of the spelling of a personal name like Psmith—a marginal note will direct his attention to the point.

If the typesetter has skipped several sentences or a longer part to do is to refer him to the original copy.

It is customary to circle numbers and words, as in 7 and seven and in mm and millimeters if you want the typesetter to "do the opposite" but be careful, for circling also means "do not set" as in the next paragraph.

Marking type specifications calls for a special language to make possible both brevity and accuracy. No publication uses all typefaces and sizes, but the most common form of a given face is called (sometimes inaccurately) *roman*. Bold face is often used for sideheads and the like. Genera and species names are printed in italic, as in Atrypa reticularis. Other special uses call for small capitals and caps and small caps, and for bold caps.

Capitals Can Be changed to lower case, and lower case to capitals.

A type character of the wrong face or size can be marked 'wrong font'. Broken or defective type should be pointed out, too.

set superscript 
and subscript 

that is not an error 

this is the end

Subscripts and superscripts, also called inferior and superior figures, occur in such things as $^{14}C_{12}$. And anything the typesetter might take to be an error, as the time term Recent, must be marked.

Finally, it helps the typesetter to use an end mark to tell him when he's finished the job.

---

key points

As your work progresses toward publication

- make as few changes as possible
- use standard symbols for copyediting
- use standard symbols for marking proofs

20 INDEXING: preparing an index

Every good book deserves a good index. A thorough index increases the value of a book; a poor or careless one detracts from its worth. Indexing is as important an art as writing, and, in some ways it is more helpful to the reader.

The difference between a well-made index and a poor one is immense. Not only is this gulf fixed between the indexes as they appear in print, but also between the quality of effort required to make them. Time is not the only ingredient that will make a good index, for indexing is not "purely clerical," as has been said. True, much clerical work is involved, but the intellectual effort is of far greater importance.

Unless you are the author of a book, you may never be asked to attempt this intellectual feat. Authors of journal articles are rarely, if ever, called upon to make indexes, although they may be asked to submit key words for the computer to use.

author as indexer

Many publishers think that the author is the best person to index a book, as he or she knows its content, its balance, its intent. "An index of superior quality in a technical work," one publisher has written, "is invariably prepared by the author himself." The American Standards Association has disagreed with this. It suggests that a professional indexer be engaged, and that this person be given credit for the work. It also urges book reviewers to comment on the absence or quality of indexes in their reviews.

Perhaps your publisher should hire a qualified professional to make your index, but the chances are slim that this will happen. If you wish, you can hire someone to prepare the index, but it is not easy to find good indexers. They are scarce and getting scarcer.

Probably you, the author, will make your own index. When you finally do, you may wish that you could start your book over, for in indexing you will discover some of the weaknesses of your work. Now—unfortunately, after it is set in type—you will find your remaining inconsistencies, perhaps even your errors. Large mistakes your publisher will no doubt allow you to correct (perhaps at your expense), but small ones you can only store away for the next edition.

aim of an index

For still another reason, you may wish you could start over. As you make an index, you must put yourself in your reader's place. Who is he? What will he want to look up? How should you help him to find it? If you are like some authors, this may be the first time you have honestly considered all of your readers. Most authors believe themselves to be thinking of their readers when they write, but exercise in indexing can make them realize how diverse their readership may be and how much their own interests have dominated their writing.

Indexing is an exercise in logic, and if your book has been logically organized, you should have few problems with your index. If, however, you find the same subject identified differently from one page to another; if you have been careless with spelling, numbers, or dates; if you have chosen "sulfur" on page 16 and "sulphur" elsewhere; if you have written "H.W. Fowler" on page 12 and "Henry W. Fowler" on page 20; if you skip from subject to subject capriciously, indexing will find you out. When you have finished, your index should have a logical, consistent, and easily recognizable pattern.

Indexes are made or completed from page proofs. You can prepare your index from the first proofs or even from the manuscript, but since the purpose of an index is to identify page numbers, it cannot be finished until page numbers are assigned.

how many indexes?

When you begin your index, ask yourself, "What is the purpose of my book?" "How will it be used?" This will help you to decide whether you need one index or several, and what sort of information you should include. If your work is chiefly bibliographic, perhaps you will need separate author and subject indexes; if yours is a botanical treatise, perhaps you need a separate index of generic and specific names.

But beware of too many indexes. Except for such special circumstances as those mentioned, most readers —as well as the American Standards Association—prefer a general index where all entries are alphabetized together.

Most professional indexers start by making a small card or paper slip for each entry. For subentries, repeat the main entry; later you will remove the repetition. Figure 31 shows a series of cards prepared for an index. Here, the information has been alphabetized and grouped, with subheadings arranged in alphabetical order. The information crossed out is the heading needed to alphabetize and sort the cards, but which will not be repeated in typing the final copy. Until alphabetization and final typing are completed, the heading should remain.

style

The precise style of index varies from publisher to publisher. By the time you are ready to make your index, you will, of course, know your publisher. Probably he will already have given you information on how to prepare the index; follow the instructions carefully.

selecting entries

Precisely what to index is your decision. Index what is important; yet bear in mind that something unimportant to you may be exactly the information someone else is seeking. Here are a few general rules: index place names; index personal names in full, whether or not that is how they appear in the text; index photographs, drawings, graphs, charts, and tables; index footnotes and appendixes if they are substantive. You will have to decide whether to index bibliographies, glossaries, and bibliographic footnotes. Use cross-references freely ("Engine, diesel"; "Diesel engine"). Be consistent in using singular or plural terms ("Paleozoic rock" or "Paleozoic rocks").

Don't overload your index with unnecessary entries; if a reference is made merely in passing, or if it is generally known, omit it. Concentrate on the significant and new contributions you have to make. Similarly, don't enter the same reference under several broad headings. In fact, you may not need very broad headings at all. For example, an index for a book entitled "Geology, Mineralogy, and Paleontology of the Pacheco Pass Quadrangle" would not need extensive listings under "Paleontology," "Mineralogy,"

"Geology," and "Pacheco Pass," just as in a book on working dogs, "Dog" would be an unnecessary entry.

Once you have selected a significant statement, make an entry that is one the reader might logically select to search. A reader seeking information on electric heaters will probably expect to find them listed under "Heaters, electric."

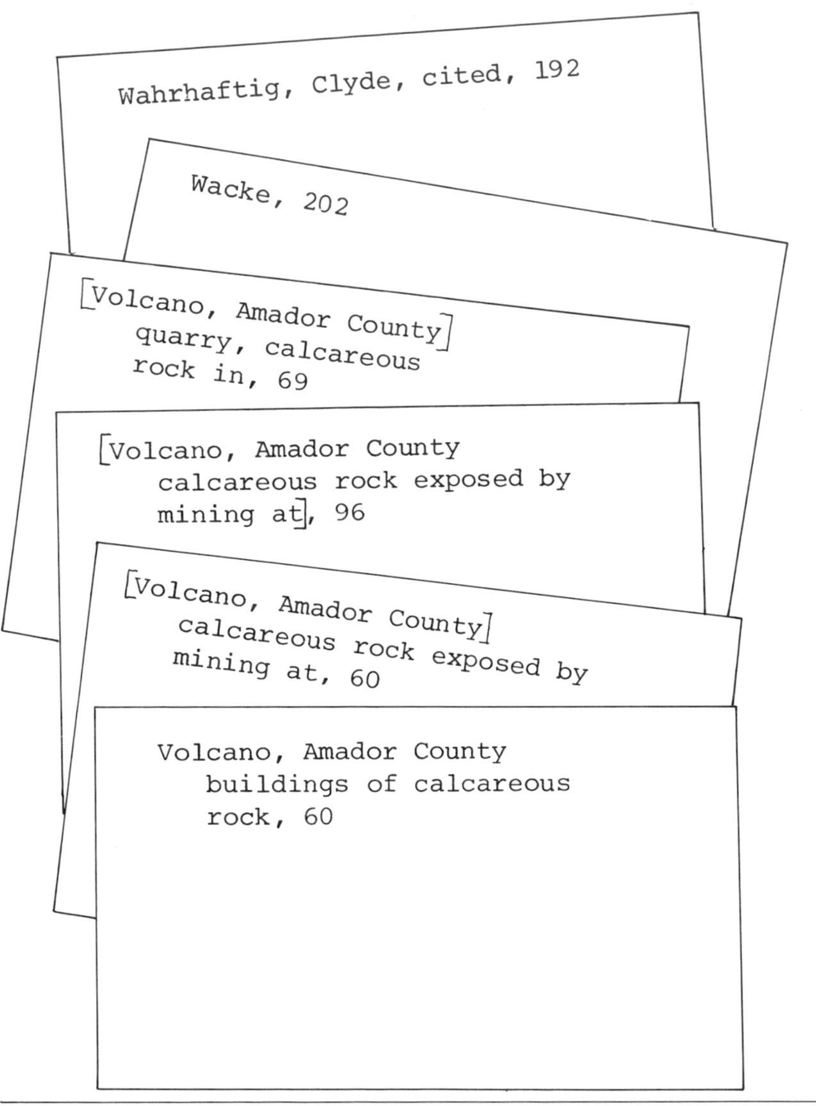

FIGURE 31 Cards prepared for final typed copy of index. Material in brackets will be omitted from the final typing. Note that the subheadings in this index will be alphabetized.

If you have several entries on one subject, such as electric appliances, you may wish to group them under "Appliances, electric," in which case you will probably have "Heaters" as a subentry and a cross-reference: "Heaters, electric. *See* Appliances, electric." If there are but one or two references to electric heaters, you would serve the reader by listing them under both "Heaters, electric" and "Appliances, electric."

For the reader's benefit, you may wish to suggest headings for him to consider. This can be done by a "See also" reference: under "Heaters, electric," enter "Heaters, electric. *See also* Appliances, gas."

key words

Select significant key words as entries—generally nouns, not adjectives. "Grades of bog-iron ore" should probably be indexed under "ore", not "grades." This item, like many others, would require more than one key word. "Iron ore, bog," might be an additional entry. Choice of key words depends, of course, upon the subject of the book, its scope, and its organization. Perhaps some key words do not appear in the text of the book, yet they are truly the subject. If so, you will need to supply them in the index.

Since a long listing of page numbers is annoying to a reader, who will have to look up each one to find the information he seeks, the most useful index has subheadings. Use no more than two orders of subheadings. If you have more than two, it is easy for the reader to get lost; also, it is difficult to set in type in narrow index columns.

alphabetizing entries

When you have completed your index cards, alphabetize them. Surprisingly, there are varying styles of alphabetization. For example, some people put "Mc" ahead of "M"; some put "Mc" and "Mac' together as if all were spelled "Mac"; others mix "Mc" and "Mac" together ahead of "M"; still others use strict alphabetization of "Mc" and "Mac" within the "M" category, using "See also" references to the other spelling. If your publisher has rules about alphabetizing, follow them; if not, we suggest these:

1. Alphabetize all entries strictly by the first solid word, disregarding articles, prepositions, and conjunctions "the"—unless part of a proper name—"and," "in," "an," "of," "for"). This will make "Mt. Whitney" appear as "Mt." not "Mount" and "St. John" appear as "St." not "Saint." A cross-reference from "Mount" and "Saint" will help.
2. In chemical terms, disregard the prefix symbol or number ("*d*-Fructose" under "F").

Cross reference used instead of page numbers	Volcanic dome. *See* Dome, volcanic
	Volcanic dust, 101-102
	Volcanic features, table of, 121-123
Subentries not capitalzed	Volcanic landscape features, drawing of, 109
	Volcanic mud flow, 104-108
	Volcanic rock, metamorphosed, 53, 60; map of, 103; table of, 119-120
	Volcanic sand, 101
Entry repeated when subject changed	Volcano, 100-123; as source of magma, 67-68; examples of, 121
	Volcano, Amador County, calcareous rock exposed by mining at, 60, 96; buildings of calcareous rock, 60; quarry, calcareous rock in, 59
	Wacke, 202
	Wahrhaftig, Clyde, cited, 192
	Walcott cirque, Antarctica, 131
	Walker Creek, till near, 155
	Walker Lake, moraines, 146, 153, 154; photo of, center section
Proper noun capitalized	Washington Column, glacial polish on, 158
	Wax, derived from coal, 90
	Wehrlite, 202
	Yosemite domes. *See* Domes, granitic
	Yosemite Falls, 135; photo of, cover
Subentries listed in order of appearance	Yosemite National Park, feldspar in domes of, 18; metamorphic rock in, 58; domes in, 73-74; granite in, 75, 78; diorite in, 78; porphyry at, 79; jade near, 83; in Tertiary time, 91; glaciers in, 131-135; drawings of, 137, 138, 139-141; ash bed in, 146; glaciers in, 150; glacial erratics in, 152; perched boulders in, 154; till in, 155; glacial moulin in, 158; glacial polish in, 158; glacial stairway in, 159; hanging valleys in, 159-160; photos of, cover, center section.
Additional references listed at end	*See also* Domes, granite; Yosemite Falls; Yosemite Valley; various Mts.

FIGURE 32 Example of an index with subheadings listed in consecutive numerical order.

3. Treat numbers as if they are written out, or write them out for main headings ("One hundred," under "O"); in subheadings, place numbers in numerical or chronological order.
4. If your entry consists of more than one word, alphabetize word by word rather than letter by letter ("New York" before "Newark"). You can, of course, use the other style, but if the index is long, you should include a note at the beginning stating which style you used.
5. Deviate from strict alphabetization when reasonable ("Henry II" before "Henry IV").
6. Make cross references to abbreviated words "National Aeronautics and Space Administration. *See* NASA").
7. Alphabetize elisions as printed, ignoring punctuation ("Who's Who" as if written "Whos Who").
8. Treat hyphenated words as separate units.

Be consistent, not only in alphabetization and spelling, but also in order of entry and punctuation. Here is a common form of entry, in which subheadings are alphabetized:

Granite, 174-181; 215-276
  in Boulder batholith, 190
  inclusions in, 47

or, this entry can be written:

Granite, 174;181; 215-276; inclusions in,
  47; in Boulder batholith, 190

Both styles are in common use. The American Standards Association recommends that subheadings be alphabetized—certainly for library use. If your publisher has not asked you to prepare subheadings in the order in which they appear in the text, follow the ASA recommendation.

typing

When you have completed and alphabetized your index, and when you have eliminated repetition, consolidated entries, and arranged punctuation, you are finally ready to type. As most indexes are set in narrow columns and small type, the temptation is great to singlespace the final typed copy. Yield not! All entries should be double- or triple-spaced. If you alphabetize subheadings, as the ASA recommends, indent the subheadings two spaces. If lines run over, indent runover lines five spaces to differentiate them from subheadings. If possible, do not start a new page in the middle of an entry; if it cannot be avoided, repeat the entry with "continued" following.

Be sure to proofread your index thoroughly, especially page numbers. It is best, at this point, to read the typed copy for spelling, and to look up each number in the page proof. This serves as a check of your original work, as well as of the newly typed copy.

computer indexing

It may be that you will never be asked to provide a handmade index such as we have just described. If you write only technical papers, journal articles, or reports, all indexing of your papers may be done by someone else, or partly or wholly by machine.

The principle used in machine indexing is the same as for hand indexing: topics and subtopics are selected and entered into the index through a machine (computer). This is, of course, little different from a handmade index, where topics are selected and pass through a machine (a typewriter). Of course, the computer can alphabetize; the typewriter cannot. The ultimate aim of this kind of indexing is to avoid any hand effort—let the machine do all the work.

Ideally, the computer could scan a book, select important topics in a "hierarchical" order, enter them in its bank by page number, and produce, nearly instantaneously, an index. As yet, this ideal has not been reached. You, the author, may be asked to help toward this end by providing key words (perhaps selected from a list provided by the publisher) or by indexing your paper or report by use of a thesaurus.

thesauri

A thesaurus, for computer indexing, is a set of words ("descriptors," "terms") for use in indexing. They are artificially brief entries that serve as major headings; synonyms cannot be used. Quite a few thesauri for use in machine indexing have been built. One of these is the *Thesaurus of Engineering and Scientific Terms: A List of Engineering and Related Scientific Terms and Their Relationships for Use as a Vocabulary Reference for Indexing and Retrieving Technical Information.* Using it or any of the many other specialized ones, an indexer can construct more detailed breakdowns of special fields, thereby creating an even more specialized, computer-oriented thesaurus.

By selecting the terms that apply to your book or paper in a specific hierarchy, you can provide the input for a

```
ıctase and   CYTOCHROME c reductase were
sulting in   CYTOCHROME c that was still
orse HEART   CYTOCHROME c treated with Sa
TIVITY of    CYTOCHROME c was influenced
alicylated   CYTOCHROME c was no longer a
containing   CYTOCHROME c were significan
er mole of   CYTOCHROME c, which contains
EFFECT OF    CYTOCHROME c.=
kidase and   CYTOCHROME oxidase increased
ı at which   CYTOCHROME oxidase was comple
ssibly the   CYTOCHROME oxidases were inve
ON via the   CYTOCHROME PATHWAY increases
hrough the   CYTOCHROME SYSTEM in the ribo
, Quinone,   CYTOCHROMES, and possibly the
```

Carboxymethyl benzyl cellulose	27
Carboxymethyl cellulose	36
Casting blades	2
Catalysts	6
Catalysts, basic sulfate	
Catalysts, cation-active	36
Cation-exchange resins, sulfonated	6
synthetic	52
Cation-active catalysts	52
Cellulose, alkali	52
Cellulose, alkali benzyl	
Cellulose, alkali epichlorohydrin	52
Cellulose, alkali epichlorohydrin benz-	52
yl	52
Cellulose, carboxymethyl	52
Cellulose, carboxymethyl benzyl	52

$C_{15}H_{19}ClN_4$	O	$\cdot 2HCl$
$C_{11}H_{14}Cl_2$	O	
$C_{15}H_{19}Cl_2N_5$	O	$\cdot HCl$
$C_{10}H_{21}IN_2$	O	
$C_{17}H_{18}K$	O	
$C_{17}H_{18}Li$	O	
$C_5H_{13}N$	O	
$C_{10}H_{21}N$	O	
$C_5H_{14}N$	O	$\cdot Cl$
$C_{10}H_{20}N$	O	$\cdot Cl$
$C_5H_{14}N$	O	PS_2
$C_5H_{14}N$	O	$PS_2 \cdot \frac{1}{2}Ni$
$C_{10}H_{21}N$	O	Pb
$C_5H_{13}N$	O	S
$C_{10}H_{21}N$	O	S

FIGURE 33

Three kinds of index produced wholly or partly by computer. At top, left, is an example of a KWIC (Key Word In Context) index. Each title or sentence in an abstract is rotated about each significant word; each word is then printed in alphabetical order, together with the surrounding words (context).

More conventional, less voluminous, and easier to read is the second index (left, bottom), compiled and printed by computer, but based on terms selected by an indexer.

At right is a sample of a wholly new index created entirely by computer. This is the HAIC (Hetero-Atom-In-Context) index, which extends the KWIC concept to molecular formulas.

All examples are from publications of Chemical Abstracts Service, whose computer-based operation, which includes all operations from indexing to printing, is the most advanced in the world.

computer-made index, or allow your paper to be cited ("retrieved") by machine as a possible source document for someone interested in the subjects you have covered.

Whether you are asked to work with a thesaurus or not, two parts of your publication are critical to present computer-based systems: the title and the abstract. Certainly, the title will be used to determine content; in some systems, retrieval provides the title of a paper (or the subject) and a "display" of the contents—very often, the author's abstract. If the abstract does not reflect the contents accurately, readers ("users") who need the information may not elect to read the paper and thereby miss significant information.

digging deeper

Most published information on indexing is aimed at indexing libraries, not books. Some publishers provide instructions to authors that include suggestions on indexing. If your publisher does not give you the company's house rules, a good reference is Robert L. Collison's *Indexes and Indexing* (4th edition, 1972; Ernest Benn, London, and John De Graff, New York). His subtitle gives the plot away: *Guide to the Indexing of Books, and Collections of Books, Periodicals, Music, Recordings, Films, and Other Material, with a Reference Section and Suggestions for Further Reading.*

A very useful booklet with an American bias is *Indexing: Principles, Rules, and Examples* by Martha Thorne Wheeler (New York State Library, 1957). The American Standards Association has published *American Standard Basic Criteria for Indexes* (revised, 1968), which gives its recommendations on alphabetizing and indexing. A companion pamphlet is the British Standards Institution's *Recommendations for the Preparation of Indexes for Books, Periodicals, and Other Publications* (1964; British Standards Institution). Its *Alphabetical Arrangement* (1968) gives rules on alphabetization for all kinds of indexes and catalogs.

For information on computer indexing, a good reference to consult is *MAMMAX,: Machine-made and Machine-aided Index* (National Federation of Science Abstracting and Indexing Services, Annual Meeting, Philadelphia, March, 1967, published by Southwest Research Institute, Applied Mechanics Reviews Report no. 45, 1968).

key points

In indexing

- be thoughtful
- be consistent
- be logical
- be thorough
- consider your readers' needs

21 ADVERTISING: writing advertising copy and press releases

author's view

Advertising in the usual sense of print advertising in magazines and journals is the publisher's responsibility, and naturally most authors prefer to leave it that way. Yet authors are notorious for complaining that their books are not selling well and that the reason is the publisher's failure to advertise. Sometimes the authors are right, but you must remember that your publisher wants sales and income at least as much as you do. If your publisher's marketing people think that advertising your book will result in enough sales to repay the cost, you can be sure that they will buy space and place ads.

publisher's view

You may be able to help by suggesting journals commonly read by people you know will be interested in your book's subject matter. However, check each one to make sure that it still carries advertising; and avoid padding your list with journals that are only marginally pertinent. That is, take great care to maintain your credibility.

jacket blurbs

Jacket blurbs, which are printed on the inside flaps and the back of the dust jacket, make excellent point-of-sale advertising. Reviewers find them useful, too, for an over-all view before digging into the book itself.

checking copy

Unfortunately, the author seldom either writes the blurb or checks its copy, and sometimes embarrassing errors result. Tell your publisher that you are willing to check copy for jacket blurbs, but in checking them confine yourself to the facts unless you happen to have some background in promotion or advertising.

press releases The overriding purpose of a press release is to inform its readers, whoever they are. Its first reader is most likely to be an editor who will decide whether to print it, rewrite it, or use information from it as the starting point for an entirely new story. If the release concerns a new book, it may determine whether the book will be listed or reviewed—or ignored.

Let's say you are to write a release to publicize a colleague's new book. First, ask yourself: Where will we send this release? Until you can answer specifically, do not write anything.

In this example, the most likely answer will consist of editors of specific journals in your field and perhaps of writers in the book-review departments of certain newspapers. Here you should consider writing more than one release, each tailored to the needs and interests of different editors or groups of editors.

In one sense you are reviewing the book, with the disadvantage of being known to be biased in its favor. For that reason you must prefer facts to opinion and news to praise. Search for the news—whatever sets the book apart and makes it noteworthy; do not take refuge in the dreary although admittedly factual recital so common in announcements of new books: "Contra Costa Press, of Oakland, California, has published a new book entitled *Flora and Fauna of Grizzly Peak,* by Wendy Dipper. The book has 309 pages and 25 figures, several of them photographs in full color, and it costs $9.95 plus 6 percent sales tax in California."

finding the news Again, find the news: Is the subject topical, as fluorocarbons versus the ozone layer would have been in the mid-1970s? Is the author's approach unusual? Are the conclusions striking? Did the work that preceded writing involve unusual procedures or out-of-the-way places? Will the book's readers be able to apply the information in their own work?

Begin with news, stick to facts, and leave statistics until later. Answer the questions likely to be asked by someone who has never seen the book.

typing Abide by all the usual rules for preparing a typescript: doublespace throughout; double check all facts, numbers, and spelling; type on one side of the paper only. Also, give your name, address, and telephone number—yours, or those of another reliable source of more information about the topic.

Be sure to mark any photographs you send with the press release. Fasten all pages together (loose sheets annoy editors), and include the date—especially if you want a line like this: HOLD FOR RELEASE APRIL 1, 1979.

proofreading

Finally, proofread the release carefully, and ask a third person (not the typist) to read it, too. Few things are so hard to correct as a faulty press release that has been mailed.

reviews

Reviews are the cheapest form of advertising for books and may be the most effective. For little more than the production cost of a single copy (perhaps a fifth of the retail price) the publisher may get in return a review filling a page that, if bought for advertising space, would cost several hundred dollars. Also, the copywriting and the typesetting are free to the publisher, and there is no commission to pay to an advertising agency. Finally, almost any review will result in sales; in fact, it has been argued that there is no such thing as a bad review.

appropriate journals

Your publisher may ask you to suggest technical journals that are likely to be interested in reviewing your book. Of course you will be familiar with the journals in your specialty, but take care to check recent copies of each one to make certain that it actually carries book reviews.

listings

Do not feel hurt if a journal merely lists your book in its new-books section instead of reviewing it. After all, many books are competing for the space, and perhaps a full review may appear later; many librarians—and ordinary readers—skim such lists. Also, you can encourage listings and reviews, too, by writing an informative foreword and introduction and by helping the publisher produce a useful jacket blurb.

display copies

Display copies also help sales. Here, too, you can help your publisher by suggesting that he exhibit publications at technical meetings in your field, but be sure that the meetings you propose do include commercial exhibits.

digging deeper

How to Advertise (Kenneth Roman and Jane Maas, 1976; St. Martin's Press, New York) is described precisely by its subtitle: *A*

Professional Guide for the Advertiser. What Works. What Doesn't. And Why. This is really for the advertiser—that is, your publisher—but it's highly readable and will help you understand how services and products, including books, are promoted. Also try *Confessions of an Advertising Man* (David Ogilvy, 1972; Ballantine Books, New York) for an individual point of view by an innovative professional. Although these books are aimed at advertising people, you can use the advice in your own writing.

key points

Help your publisher sell your work by

- suggesting places to advertise
- checking jacket blurbs
- writing a press release
- sending releases to editors most likely to use them
- seeking out news and sticking to facts
- double spacing, double checking, and proofreading

22 SPEAKING: presenting speeches and giving interviews

After your book is published, you may be invited to be a guest lecturer or after-dinner speaker, or you may be interviewed on radio or television. But even if your book remains only in your mind, you, as a scientist or engineer, will be called upon to speak many times in the course of your career. Probably you have already presented the findings on which your article was based before an audience of your peers; if you have written a textbook, no doubt your students have had early feasts on the material in it. You have passed these hurdles, but there are more to come. You will have new results to report to your colleagues, new lectures to give to your classes, and you may be asked for more popular presentations to audiences not trained in your specialty.

help from the pros

If you are asked to give a radio lecture or a television interview, we have but few words of advice. Members of the staff of the station will assist you in preparation. They will help you decide what to wear, and help you with what to say. When you speak, speak slowly. Treat your subject succinctly yet fully. All of us have watched the spectacle of an expert being led by an interviewer, who is, in truth, interviewing himself:

Q. "What would you say about the magnetism of iron, Doctor Smith?"

A. "I would say that it is magnetic."

Q. "And this brown color, this rust, is it an oxide of iron, Doctor?"

A. "It is an oxide of iron."

If you can, carry the subject on yourself, so that you will not need to be so obviously "led"; be enthusiastic, but avoid "rattling on."

before the camera

Besides a natural nervousness before cameras, amateur television performers have obvious faults that you should avoid. First, sit extraordinarily still—far stiller, perhaps, than you normally would. We have all been annoyed by someone who kicks his feet or snaps his knuckles; on television such nervous habits become intolerable, and even ordinary shifting can be annoying.

Second, don't be afraid to look into the camera, but do not visibly acknowledge the presence of the many technicians (cameramen, floor managers, etc.) surrounding you. Any rapport you and the other performers have built up with the audience in the glass eye of the camera is destroyed when you acknowledge the technicians. Remember that people in the audience cannot see them and feel left out; it is as if you and the staff had private secrets (which, of course, is true; they will be giving you timing and other cues).

slide talks

Whether or not you become a television success, you will surely give formal papers, speeches, and talks. Probably these will be illustrated; the "slide talk" is nearly as common in our society as the automobile. But you need not necessarily use slides for an illustrated talk: you can use film, but if you do, you must time your speech exactly with it or the impact is lost. Or, you can give a "chalk" or "feltboard" talk, if your audience is small enough. All these methods require special talent or preparation. Film must, of course, be taken, edited, and printed; felt cutouts must be prepared well in advance, and chalk talks are successful only if the speaker has considerable artistic ability. Both feltboards and blackboards are visible only to a small audience, such as a school class.

Chances are you will elect to show projected illustrations. Here, as in all public displays of your work, nothing will help you more than adequate preparation. You have already spent months, perhaps years, of your life on the research that has brought you to this point; now add the extra effort necessary to give a professional presentation.

Select your slides carefully. Make certain that each one adds to the audience's knowledge. Try to vary them, using close-ups, long shots, and medium shots intermingled in a meaningful way.

In some places, you may wish to insert title shots, or a few words of explanation—especially if the subject is unfamiliar or the words difficult or foreign. These can be interspersed with shots of objects to give variety and clarity. All "titles" do not need to go at the beginning or the end.

charts

If you use charts or graphs, consider a "progressive" chart—one in which the pieces are added as you talk about them. This requires several slides showing pieces of the same chart (see Figure 34). You may also need more than one copy of a slide. If you intend to discuss the same slide at different places in your presentation, use a duplicate; don't expect the projectionist to hunt through the tray to find the correct slide.

story boards

Many professionals who give illustrated lectures prepare for them by using "story board" techniques. They make pencil sketches of each slide (whether they have prepared it yet or not), so that they can lay out the order of slides to find where they should add or subtract material. An assistant helping to prepare visual materials can then readily see what fits where and why.

If there are brief points in your discussion where you have no slides, add a blank—a cardboard cut to slide size or a piece of black film. Otherwise, the bright projection light will startle and distract your audience. It is better to talk to a darkened screen than to leave an already discussed slide on the screen, or to show a new one for your audience to wonder about.

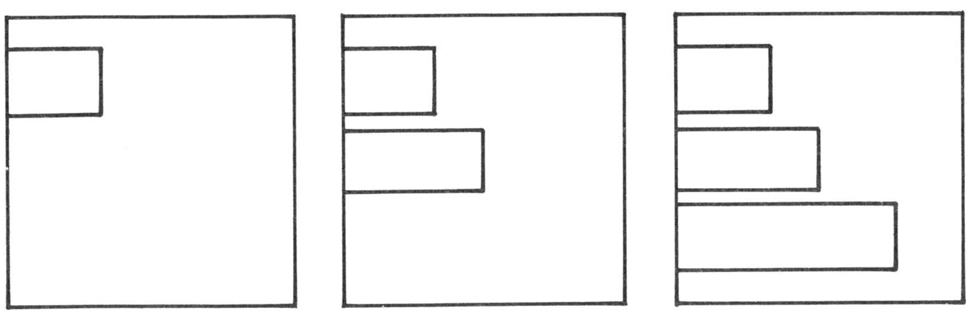

FIGURE 34 How three consecutive slides could be used to emphasize information on a chart.

When you have determined the order of all of your slides, blanks included, "thumb spot" them in the lower left-hand corner. If you use white thumb spots, you can also number the slides in proper sequence on the thumb spot. You may also be asked to furnish a title card, giving the sequence and subject of each slide for the benefit of the projectionist.

scripts You may wish to furnish yourself with a script that shows small photos or sketches of the actual slide to be seen on the screen so that your narration will be correctly timed. It is best, of course, if you can present your lecture with a minimum of notes. Whatever you do, don't read the script. Try to present it in an interesting, yet casual, manner. Be certain that you are discussing the correct slide at all times, but talk to the audience, not the screen.

When you have mastered these techniques (some scientists do truly become masters), you may wish to move on to more challenging, perhaps more effective, techniques such as multiple screen presentations or mixed media talks. Using these methods (if your program chairman can make the physical arrangements), you can show an object and its detail simultaneously, or show motion, or multiply information in a very striking way. Used poorly, or without proper planning, such complex arrangements deteriorate into an upsetting experience for the audience; used effectively, they are outstanding.

key points

If you speak in public

- speak slowly and naturally
- treat your subject succinctly yet fully
- prepare illustrations carefully

23 SHOWING: selecting a projector

Several kinds of projectors can be used to illuminate still images: of these, the opaque projector, the overhead projector, and the transparency projector are most common. Which of these you will be able to use depends upon which are available to you, the type of material you intend to display, and the size of your audience.

opaque projector

The opaque projector can project illustrations that are not transparent, and are less than 11 inches (28 cm) square. It is the only one of the standard projectors that can show copy from printed books, magazines, photographs, or maps. Since it cannot project an image larger than 8 feet wide and must be positioned near the screen, it is not suitable for large audiences. Unless you speak directly from the projector, you will need the help of a projectionist.

overhead projector

A newer kind is the overhead projector, which illuminates images from transparent copy that is 10 inches square (some less common overhead projectors use other sizes of copy). Unlike the opaque projector, the overhead projector is most effective when operated by the speaker. Transparencies to be used in this projector can be prepared from black-and-white or colored copy on clear plastic film. As the illustration can be altered or drawn by the speaker using a grease pencil during the lecture, this form of projection is very effective when used by a master showman.

Both the opaque and overhead projectors require you to position the copy carefully; audiences can be confused when the slides are changed or the copy is shifted. On the whole, these two projectors are more suitable for schoolroom use than for formal presentations before large audiences.

transparency (slide) projector

The most common projector used today is one that illuminates prepared transparencies that are inserted into the machine vertically (parallel to the screen). Many of us have our own slide projectors of this type. For many years, the standard slide was a 3½- by 4-inch glass slide that could be used to project either photographs or art work. Schools and professional organizations still have this kind of projector, but few individuals own them. Their use is declining.

glass slides

Slides for projection by this machine are usually made on sensitized glass positive-image plates. They can be made by contact printing or enlargement from any black-and-white negative, to produce a black-and-white slide. They have the disadvantage of being extremely fragile: as the emulsion is on the glass itself, if the slide is dropped or improperly ventilated when projected, it will break, destroying the image.

You can, of course, make slides of this size by using transparency film in a large format camera, then trimming it to size, or you can make a positive or a negative (white on black) transparency for use in a projector of this size. You will have to mount films made by either of these techniques in glass, as cardboard-mounted slides warp excessively.

instant slides

The Polaroid Corporation has developed a system of making slide materials of this size in the camera. Film exposed in this way can be mounted in plastic without cover glasses, but is not suitable for use in high-intensity projectors without a ventilated glass protective cover. Such slides have the advantage of speedy preparation, but do not let the ease of preparation cause you to lower your standards for quality.

35 mm slides

Although there are projectors and slides in other sizes, the most common kind now used for transparency projection is the "35 millimeter" projector and slide. Most 35 mm slides ("35 mm" refers to the width of the film) are made directly in the camera, by exposing a roll of color film. Emulsion-coated glass is available to make black-and-white slides; you can also make black-and-white slides by using black-and-white film, or by photographing black-and-white copy on color film. A positive image (black on white) will

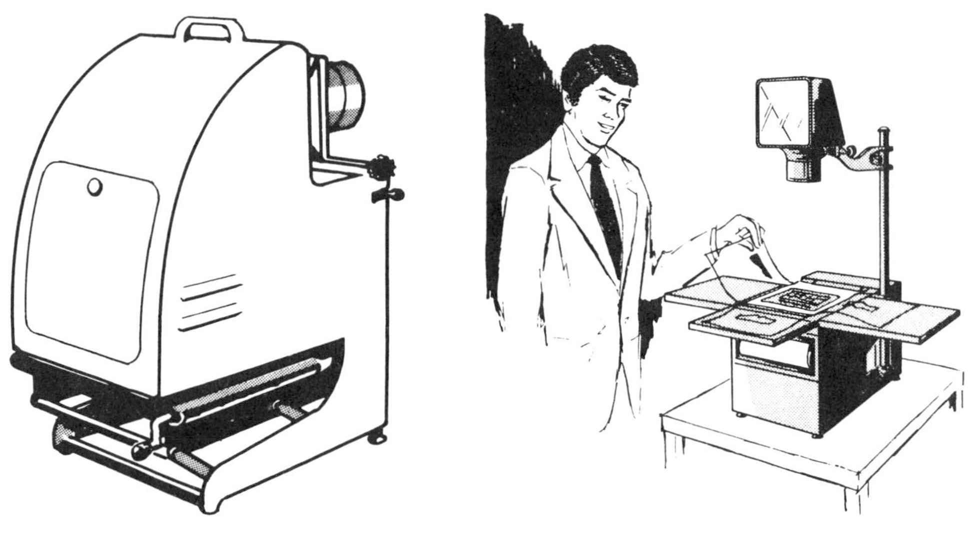

FIGURE 35

Three kinds of projectors are in common use. Top, left, is an opaque projector, which will show material from printed books; right, an overhead projector, which allows the lecturer to manipulate the projector while speaking; bottom, a professional 35mm arc projector.

result from using direct positive films, special polyester film (such as DuPont "Cronaflex"), or by making a negative from a negative. Not all film is suitable for this purpose. Only very fine-grained film, such as Eastman Kodak Panatomic or Kodalith, will give sharp results. Polaroid film is available in this size, too, for preparing slides rapidly.

mounting slides

Some scientific organizations, who use professional carbon-arc projectors that may have projection lamps as bright as 3,000 watts, specify that no cardboard mounts can be used at professional meetings. All slides must be mounted in glass. To achieve this with slides that have emulsion on glass, you need only add a cover glass and binding tape. To mount slides consisting of pieces of sandwiched film, you need two layers of glass.

In mounting, beware of the binding tape. Ordinary drafting tape cannot be used, as it ages rapidly in heat to become hard, losing its adhesiveness. Plastic and cloth tape that has been sold as "slide binding tape" is effective when new, but with age it becomes excessively gummy, eventually reaching a stage so sticky that it cannot be inserted in the projector. Heavy paper tape, such as is used in libraries, is useful, but transparent plastic tapes are not usable. Metal and plastic mounts are perhaps more durable, but they are not usable unless vented.

Those of us who have seen our favorite slides, lovingly mounted, haunted by gray, moving spectres flowing across the screen will realize the importance of ventilation. All slides using film must be ventilated, as the gelatinous nature of the film, together with moist air trapped at the time of mounting, forms unwanted clouds when heated in the projector. Eventually the clouds become permanent disfiguring additions to the slide. Only slides made from emulsion-coated glass need not be ventilated.

One other warning: remember that glass-mounted slides may be too thick for some slide trays. Never mount slides in glass without removing them from the cardboard mount furnished by the photofinisher. Slides so mounted are too thick for all projectors, and will warp during projection.

digging deeper

See page 165.

key points

Different kinds of projectors can project

- pictures from books
- drawings made on the spot
- black-and-white or color transparencies

24
TELLING: making and showing slides

Color slides, even for line work, are now used far more often than black and white. Speakers at many scientific and technical meetings, as well as those addressing lay groups, use color slides to supplement, illustrate, or present their subjects. If you take your own slides, make certain that your focus is sharp and that the exposure is accurate. If you must choose between a slight underexposure and overexposure, choose to underexpose, as a high-intensity projection light may flood an overexposed transparency into illegibility.

composition

Follow the rules of good composition. If you do not know them, find them out or ask a professional photographer to make slides for you. Whether your audience knows why your slides are bad or not, they will know that they are bad, and will judge your work—no matter how good it may be scientifically—by them.

The most common flaws in composition come from the photographer's lack of concentration on his subject. Often he is not close enough, so that the viewer is left wondering what the subject is. Or he may err by allowing another object to dominate or interfere with the subject. If possible, the subject should be lighter in tone than the rest of the photograph. Try to have lines in the photograph—whether they be trees, circulating blood, crystal twins, or whatever—arranged in such a way that they focus attention

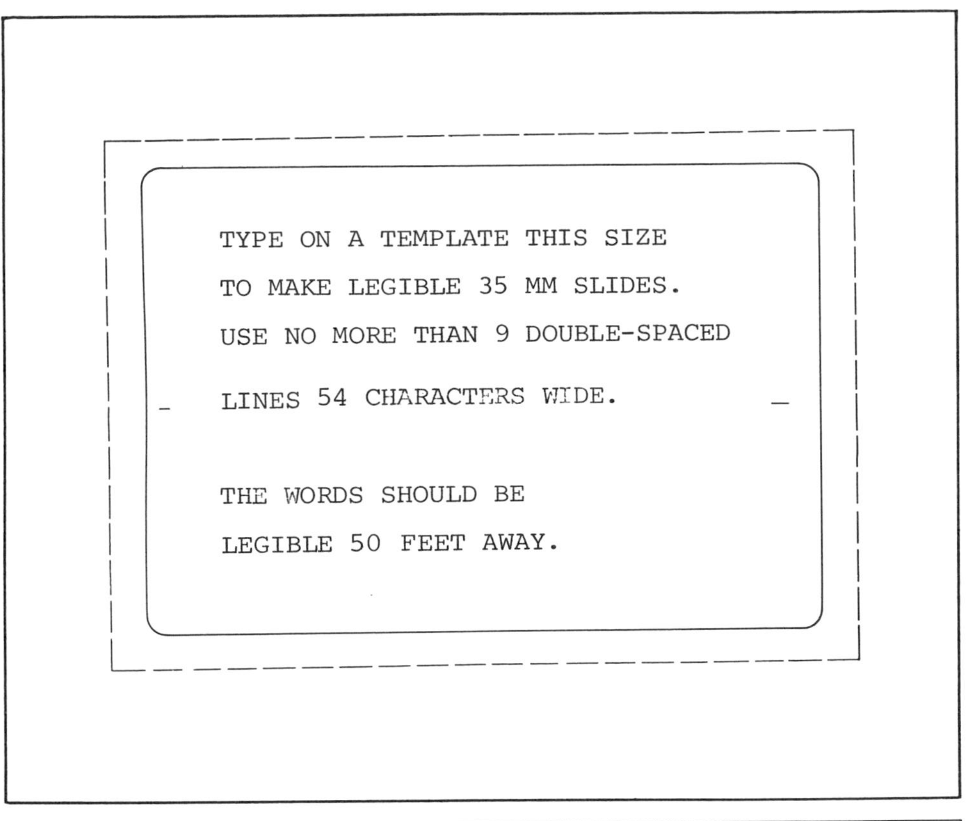

Template for making 35mm typed slides. FIGURE 36

on the subject rather than away from it. Radial lines, for example, draw attention toward the convergence. Vertical or horizontal lines, if properly used, can clarify the subject; if carelessly used, they can divide the photograph into segments that compete for the viewer's attention.

None of these rules is hard and fast. A knowledgeable artist can violate them with success. If you are not knowledgeable in art, be cautious.

Out-of-focus, poorly exposed, or badly designed photographs may disturb your audience, but most truly distressed audiences become so from attempting to understand illegible art work. It is not the "scenic" slide, but the table, the chart, the map that is most sinned against—and most used by speakers on science subjects.

For publication, most art work is reduced by perhaps as much as half. Slides, however, are enlarged by many

FIGURE 37

diameters, perhaps as much as 20 times. One would guess, knowing this, that most slides would have far too little copy to maintain viewer interest. The reverse is true. Poor slides—whose numbers are legion—most commonly attempt to show too much material. The graph in Figure 14 (page 66) is clear on the printed page, but would make a disturbing lecture slide.

legibility

Legibility depends upon the size and quality of the projected image, as well as the distance and angle of the viewer from it. To prepare excellent slides, you will need to know all of these variables: the size of the audience; the size, shape, and kind of screen; the kind of projector and its wattage. For large professional groups, or those who are not accustomed to dealing with audiovisual materials, much of the needed information may be lacking. Nevertheless, you can avoid some of the more common errors by making your work large and uncomplicated. The key to such translation is to simplify. One word is far more effective if it is visible to the entire audience than all of an illegible poem.

size of lettering

The American Standards Association provides guides for projected images, and that gives suitable line weights and lettering sizes. Eastman Kodak Company has available a "Legibility calculator" that will show the minimum letter size in original art work that will be legible to the entire audience. As these factors vary, the calculator is actually a circular slide rule. Suppose you are using a 6- by 9-inch information area, and you wish to fill a 4-foot-high screen in an auditorium whose farthest seats are 64 feet away, you can set these factors on the dials and calculate the answer to "minimum art-work letter height," which is ¼ inch—the main body of your lettering will have to be at least ¼ inch high.

If you do know the size of the auditorium, you can calculate the minimum height of the smallest letters mathematically by using this formula:

$$h = \frac{0.00262\ Ac}{P}$$

where h is the minimum height of the smallest letters on art work

A is the maximum audience distance from the screen
c is the width of the art work
P is the width of the projection of the slide mask (the usable copy area).

Be sure that all of your measurements are in the metric scale or in feet and inches; don't mix units.

simplicity

If your material is too complex for easy assimilation, use two slides rather than one. Limit each slide to one main idea. If you use words, use no more than 15 to 20, and do not use material that you do not discuss. Leave space—at least the height of one capital letter—between lines. If you have titles, do not use them to regurgitate the rest of the slide. Use a dark-colored background in preference to a light one. Light backgrounds tend to "burn out" and to show flaws clearly.

digging deeper

A great deal of information has been published on the making of slides and on the presentation of illustrated lectures. Several journals on audiovisual techniques, written especially for the audiovisual specialist or the classroom teacher, and textbooks on audiovisual methods are available at libraries. In addition, Eastman Kodak Company has published books and pamphlets dealing with many facets of slide preparation and presentation. They are listed in the yearly index published by the company. The sources listed on page 53 give information on slide photography, as well as on general photographic problems.

Many professional societies have specific instructions regarding the use of slides at scientific meetings. Consult the program

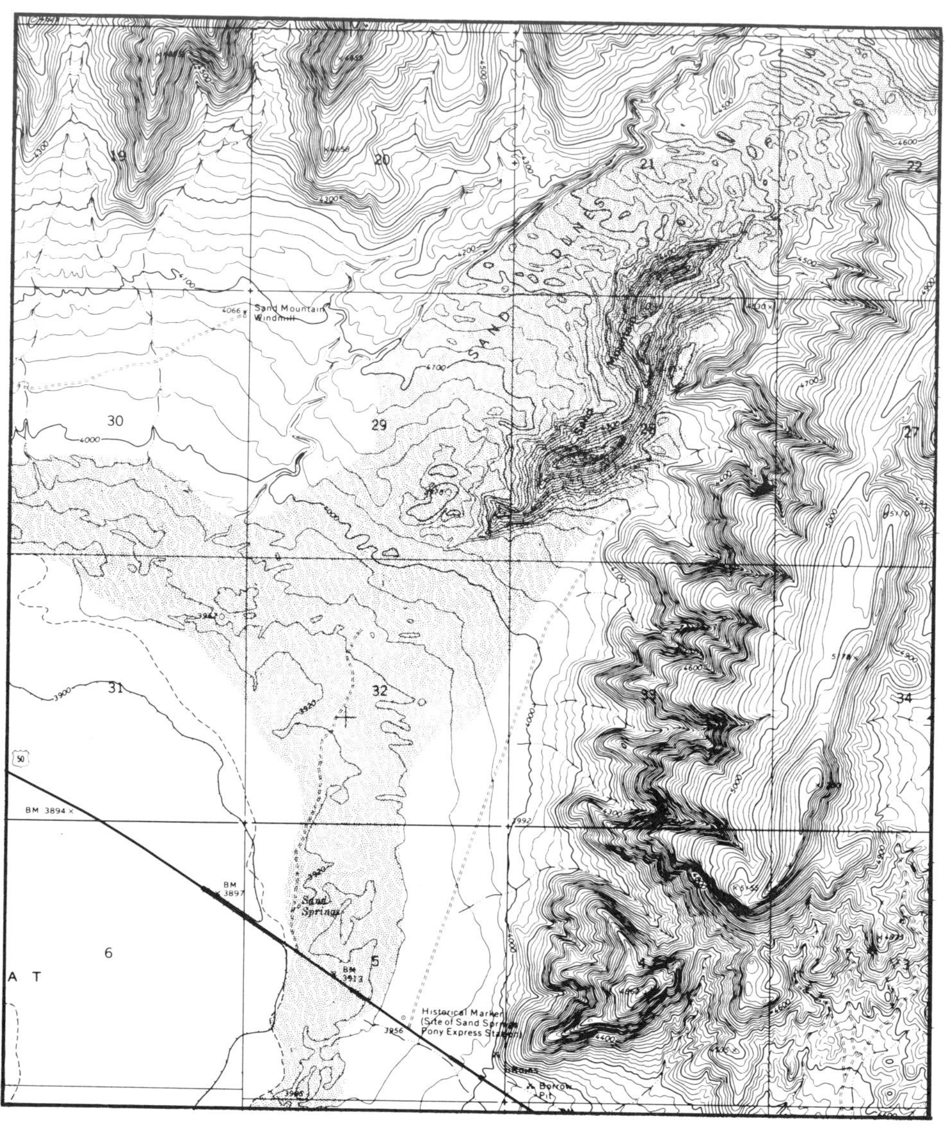

FIGURE 38 Part of a topographic map used as a book illustration. Here, a great deal of information has been shown on the printed page, where the reader can study it at leisure.

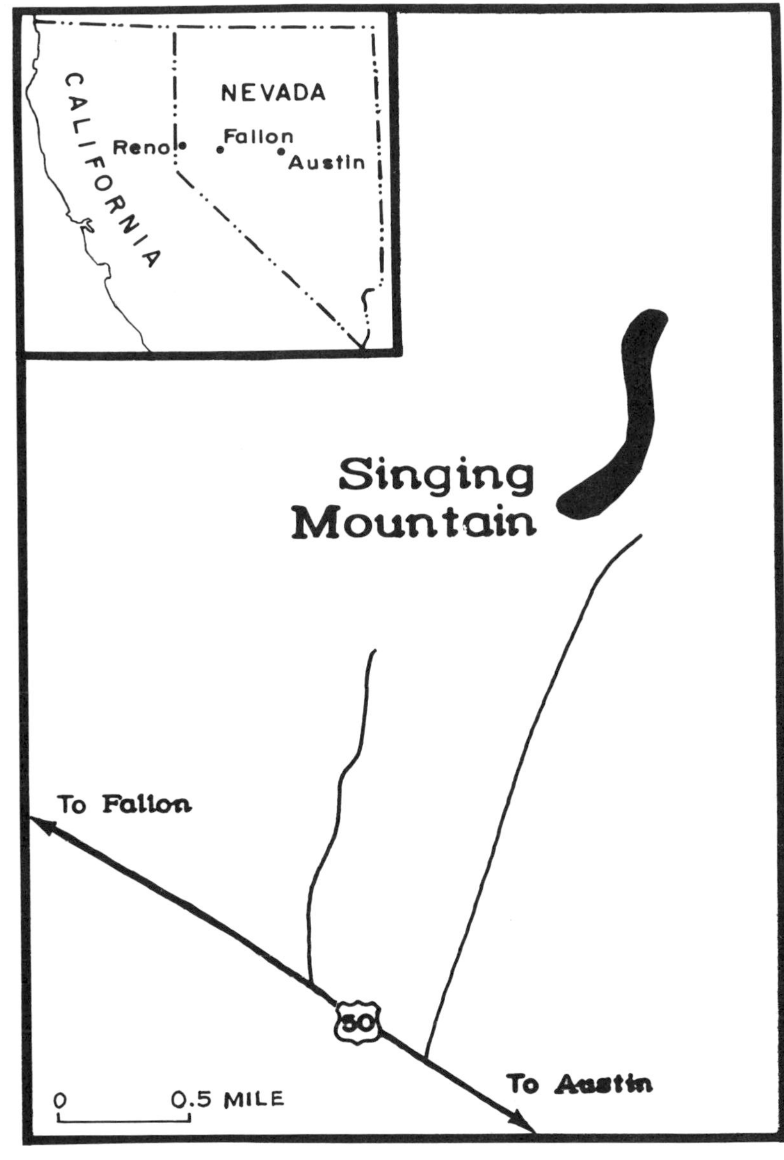

An effective slide has been made from the information in Figure 38. Here only the principal subject has been retained. The slide is visible and comprehensible in black and white; color would add interest. The original slide from which this illustration was taken was in black (the lettering and border), blue (the ocean off California in the inset figure), red (the dune), and yellow (background of all the slide except the insert, which was white).

FIGURE 39

chairman for explicit instructions and for details of the equipment available. If your slides are to be used for television broadcasting, ask the station for instructions on organizing and preparing them.

key points

In making slides to use in lectures

- follow the rules of good composition
- simplify, simplify

25 CONTINUING: beginning the next edition

author's copies

Under the terms of your contract, the publisher will give you a certain number of free copies of your book. Be sure to keep one copy of that edition, and one copy (at least) of each subsequent edition, for your own library. It may seem incredible now, but the time may come when you can't recall the name of your book or when you wrote it!

correction copy

Take another copy, mark it "correction copy," and set it aside in a handy place. As typographical and factual errors are called to your attention, mark them in the correction copy. It is wise to keep in close touch with your printer during various printings of the first edition (we hope there will be many) so that the smaller errors, such as misspellings, can be corrected. Sometimes a whole paragraph or page can be changed.

the next edition

You can, if you like, use this same correction copy when the time comes to make major revisions for the next edition of your book. Now is the time to think about establishing files for use in writing the next edition. No doubt there will be new advances in your field that you will want to take into account, thus making a revision mandatory after a while. A new edition will also give you a chance to tidy up the illustrations that could have been better and to rewrite those pages you do not like, as well as to bring the factual material up to date. And, of course, a new edition is a new book, which means new purchasers and new readers.

INDEX

Acknowledgments

Our thanks to Susan Moyer, Judy Russell, and Elisabeth Egenhoff, who read, criticized, and assisted with the entire text; to artists Caroline Norris and Hidekatsu Takada, and to cartographers Adrienne Morgan and Dorismae Weber, who aided us with the chapters on illustrations.

When we needed their advice, they gave it.

John Staples thoughtfully gave us ideas, encouragement, and the title for this book.

And last, we thank William Kaufmann, who picked up the ball that others dropped.

Sources of Illustrations

Figure 1, page 2, is by David Christianson, courtesy of the artist and *Bookbuilders West.*

Figure 2, page 25, and the symbols on pages 133-138 are modified from *Geowriting: a Guide to Writing, Editing, and Printing in Earth Science,* edited by Wendell Cochran, Peter Fenner, and Mary Hill, with permission of the publisher, American Geological Institute. Figure 3, page 26, is reproduced from *CBE Style Manual,* by permission of the Council of Biology Editors. Figures 4 (page 39), 5 (page 40), and 24 (page 80) are U.S. Geological Survey photos.

Figure 7 (page 56) is from a diagram prepared by Poly-Optics, Inc., Santa Ana, California, and is reproduced with their permission. Figure 8 (page 57) is from *Biological Principles,* by Burton S. Guttman; Figure 16 (page 68) is from *Chemical Principles,* by Richard B. Dickerson, Harry B. Gray, and Gilbert P. Haight, Jr. Permission was given to reproduce both figures by the publisher, W.A. Benjamin, Inc.

Figure 9 (page 58) was supplied by Rodney Bessolo, M.D., Franklin Hospital, San Francisco. Figure 10, page 59, is a reproduction of an original plant print by the artist, Ida Geary, Mill Valley, California. Figure 11 (page 60) is reproduced from *Geology of the Sierra Nevada,* by Mary Hill, with the permission of the University of California Press. Figure 14 (page 66) is from U.S. Geological Survey Professional Paper 870-A, by William E. Emmett; Figure 15 (page 67) and Figure 17 (page 69) are from U.S. Geological Survey Professional Paper 820, edited by Donald A. Brobst and Walden R. Pratt.

Figure 18 (page 70) is modified from the cover of *Research/ Development,* January, 1968. It illustrated an article by Harold K. Mintz, and is included here by permission of the publisher.

Figure 20 (page 72) is redrawn from U.S. Coastal Engineering Research Center, Corps of Engineers, Technical Memorandum 14, by John Cherry. Figure 21 (page 76) is from *Diving and Digging for Gold,* by Mary Hill, Naturegraph Publishers, Happy Camp, California.

Figure 25 (page 82) and 26 (page 83) were modified from California Division of Mines and Geology County Report 2, by W. B. Clark. Figure 27 was assembled from the legend of the Los Angeles Sheet, Geologic Map of California, also published by the California Division of Mines and Geology.

The table, Figure 28 (page 92), is modified from U.S. Bureau of Mines *Mineral Yearbook, 1972.*

Projectors shown in Figure 35 (page 159) are from American Association of Petroleum Geologists *Slide Manual,* by permission.

Slide templates in Figures 36 and 37 are presented by permission of Eastman Kodak Company, Rochester, N.Y. They are from the pamphlet "Effective Lecture Slides."

The slide shown in Figure 39 (page 167) was drawn by Adrienne E. Morgan, Oakland, California.

Designed by:
Judith McCarthy of San Mateo, California
and Information Design, Inc. of Salt Lake City, Utah

Type Specifications:
Univers Light and Universe Light Italic for the text
Heads and subheads are Pabst Extra Bold
Set on a Mergenthaler VIP Phototypesetter

Type Set by:
Type Design, Inc. of Salt Lake City, Utah

Printed by:
Consolidated Publications, Inc. of Palo Alto, California
and The Maple Press Company of York, Pennsylvania